KT-539-739

CLUBSPOTTING 2.0

STREET & CLUB CULTURE

LEARNING RESOURCES CENTRE

Havering College
of Further and Higher education

edited by
Paolo Davoli & Gabriele Fantuzzi

Happy Books

741.6

HL

18264

CLUBSPOTTING 2.0
STREET & CLUB CULTURE

23.6.2001 / 4.8.2001
chiostri di san pietro . reggio emilia. italy

promotori/promotors:

COMUNE DI REGGIO EMILIA
ASSESSORATO CULTURA E SAPERE

KOM-FUT MANIFESTO

MAFFIA CLUB

in collaborazione con/with the collaboration:

ARCI NUOVA ASSOCIAZIONE
COMITATO PROVINCIALE DI REGGIO EMILIA

INSTITUTE OF DUBBOLOGY
& MEDIA BLITZ

SARTORIA COMUNICAZIONE

artisti/artists:

DEFUMO
FUTURA 2000
MODE 2
DELTA

SATOSHI MATSUZAWA
STEFANO CAMELLINI
DARIO LASAGNI
MITCH
TOSHIO NAKANISHI
RUN WRACKE

direzione artistica/art direction:
DELICATESSEN
www.delica.it

ISBN 88-86416-27-X
© Copyright 2001
Happy Books & Kom-Fut Manifesto

© Copyright per i testi dei relativi autori,
per le immagini dei relativi detentori.
© the copyright for the texts is property
of the mentioned writers.
The copyright of the images/pictures
is property of the relative owners.

Printed in Italy by Grafiche Jolly (Modena) 2001

Satoshi Matsuzawa (© 2001 all rights reserved)

INDEX

INTRO

testo: Gabriele Fantuzzi

Il progetto Clubspotting nasce nel 1999 quando forte era la nostra volontà di uscire allo scoperto, dopo anni passati all'interno di un club, il Maffia, a proporre gruppi, DJ, situazioni insolite e quant'altro. Perché la cosidetta *"cultura del club"* che tanti trovano difficile da definire, diventa concreta quando produce oltre all'intrattenimento, materiali tangibili come riviste, libri e cataloghi, siti internet e artefatti grafici e ancora produzioni artistiche che diventano cd/compilation, dj set itineranti, eventi creati ad hoc come la rassegna letteraria *"Club Lit"*.

In questa seconda edizione l'orizzonte viene allargato al di fuori dell'Italia, focalizzando l'attenzione sulla cultura di strada, progenitrice per molti aspetti della club culture. **Clubspotting 2.0** ospita tre artisti/graffitisti tra i più apprezzati al mondo ovvero *Futura 2000*, *Mode 2* e *Delta* con il progetto **DEFUMO** realizzato interamente in Italia. I loro lavori rappresentano lo stato dell'arte, nascono nell'ambito della street culture per sconfinare in territori affini fino ad arrivare nei circuiti artistici di rilievo internazionale senza mai perdere di autenticità. Sul versante musicale viene dedicato un'approfondimento alla Pussyfoot, una delle storiche etichette indipendenti che più hanno osato sia nella ricerca sonora che nella sperimentazione visiva per merito, soprattutto, di DJ come *Howie B*, *Spacer*, *Palmskin* e art designer come *Toshio Nakanishi*, *Mitch* e *Run Wrake*.

La sezione *Flyer*Zone* ospita una selezione di artefatti grafici realizzati dalle crew di designer responsabili di quattro tra i migliori club al mondo che non appartengono geograficamente alla fascia calda di Londra, Ibiza o New York. Sono i fratelli minori e maggiori del Maffia. Si tratta di club talvolta distanti tra loro migliaia di chilometri ma animati, però, dallo stesso spirito. Sono lo **Zouk** di Singapore, il **Luxfragil** di Lisbona, il **Flex** di Vienna e l'avanguardista **Dinamo Dvash** di Tel Aviv. Visitate i loro bellissimi siti per farvi un'idea di ciò che la cultura dei club può produrre.

In *Art*Zone* presentiamo i nuovi lavori di artisti già inseriti nella prima edizione e che per la loro qualità seguiremo anche in futuro; sono l'illustratore giapponese **Sato Labo** e il visual designer **Roberto Bagatti**. Nella sezione Nu*directors, **Matteo Bittanti** si occupa di tre registi di videoclip: **Glazer**, **Sigismondi** e **Sednaoui**. Lo stesso Bittanti conclude l'opera con un saggio illustrato sui contagiosi *Dance Games* che, da tipico fenomeno giapponese, si preparano a conquistare il pubblico mondiale. Anche questa è club culture.

CLUBSPOTTING

INTRO

text: Gabriele Fantuzzi

The Clubspotting project was born in 1999, so strong was our desire to come out in the open, after past years of being inside one club, Maffia, proposing groups, DJs, unusual situations and so much more. Because it has been called a "club culture" which many be hard to define, it becomes more concrete when it produces entertainment, tangible material like magazines, books and catalogues, internet sites, graphic artefacts and other artistic productions which become CD compilations, DJ sets and other things created literally ad hoc as the literary review, "ClubLit".

In this second edition the horizon has increased to go outside of Italy, focusing attention on the street-culture, *progenitor* for many aspects of the club-culture. **Clubspotting 2.0** will host three of the most revered living artists in the world as *Futura 2000*, *Mode 2* and *Delta* with the project **DEFUMO**. Their work represents the state of the art, born in the environment of the street culture but able to cross the borders reaching the internationally renowned artistic circuits without ever losing their authenticity.
On the music side, the attention is focused on Pussyfoot, one of the historic independent labels which has sought out experimental sounds and visuals thanks above all to DJs like *Howie B*, *Spacer*, *Palmskin*, and art designers like *Toshio Nakanishi*, *Mitch Design* and *Run Wrake*.
The section *Flyer*zone* hosts a selection of graphic artefacts done by the design crew of four of the best clubs who are considered, geographically, outside the hot spots of cities like London, Ibiza and New York. They are the big and little brothers of **Maffia**. We are dealing with clubs that are thousand of kilometres away but contain the same spirit, they are **Zouk** of Singapore, **Luxfragil** of Lisbon or **Rex** of Vienna and even **Dinamo Dvash** of Tel Aviv. Visit their gorgeous web-sites to give yourself an idea of the culture that clubs can produce.
In the *Art*Zone* we present the latest work of artists already included in the first edition and who, as a result of their quality, will be followed in the future as well; they are the Japanese illustrator **Sato Labo** and the visual designer **Roberto Bagatti**.
In the section of Nu*directors, Matteo Bittanti ventures upon describing three videos: *Glazer*, *Sigismondi* and *Sednaoui*. The same Bittanti concludes the catalogue with an illustrated essay on the catching and contagious *Dance Games* that, beginning from a typical Japanese phenomenon, are ready to conquer the world-wide audience... This, too, is club culture.

LA LIBERTÀ DI ESSERE LIBERI

di Paolo Davoli

Ironia.

La miglior definizione della famiglia-etichetta Pussyfoot è una frase del poeta italiano Angelo Maria Ripellino quando, citando i futuristi russi come Majakovskij, li definisce affettuosamente "Barnum d'avanguardia". Ogni qualvolta mi avvicino a una opera Pussyfoot, automaticamente mi ricordo di quella frase e ciò mi procura nell'animo un malizioso e complice sorriso. "*Chissà anche questa volta cosa avranno inventato, quali giochi pirotecnici avranno attivato...*" è il mio solitario pensiero. Perchè, se una caratteristica può balzare in evidenza nelle composizioni pussyfootiane, quella certamente principale è l'ironia. Dalle tematizzazioni delle raccolte, che passano con lievità dall'icona filmica di James Bond ai temi della pornografia e dai fumetti al cartografare nuovi luoghi musicali quali il Giappone, le tracce disvelano sempre un approccio umoristico alla composizione.

Il suono quindi come portato umoristico, come "battuta" musicale, come "follia" delirante, alterante la realtà quotidiana. Squarci musicali che sembrano recuperare l'ironia astratta e geniale dei **fratelli Marx** ci proiettano in un universo musicale dove non esiste confine, periferia, separazione tra popolare e sperimentazione, tra codice e *freeform*, tra ritornello e astratto. Bruciati sotto l'altare di una comunicazione attonita e surreale vi sono i generi musicali: rock, jazz, ambient, hip hop perdono di significato semantico. Non esiste orizzonte codificato nel "Barnum d'avanguardia" Pussyfoot. Liberi dalle costrizioni vincolanti. Liberi di essere liberi. L'ironia quindi come pratica liberante. D'altra parte alcune civiltà arcaiche non credevano forse che una "risata cosmica" fosse alle scaturigini del mondo?

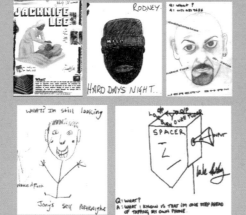

kate harrison

THE FREEDOM OF BEING FREE

by Paolo Davoli

Irony.

The best definition for the family-label Pussyfoot is a phrase from an Italian poet Angelo Maria Ripellino when, citing Russian futurists like Majakovskij, he affectionately defines them as the *Barnum of avant-garde*. Every time I get close to a work of art by Pussyfoot, that line automatically returns at my mind and it brings a feathery smile from my soul. "*Who knows, this time, what they have invented... which pyrotechnic games they have activated...*" this is my usual thought. Because if there is a characteristic that one can slide into evidence from the composition it is certainly irony. From the themes of stories, told lightly through the film icon James Bond to the themes of pornography, from cartoons to the cartography of new places/spaces where to hear music as Japan, the tracks always show a humorous approach and a conscious knowledge of their resounding madness. The sound, therefore like a humorous experience, like delirious lunacy, like musical "joke", altering daily life. Musical scores, that seem to recover the abstract irony and genius of the Marx brothers, lunch us out in a musical universe where there are no confines, periphery, or separation between the popular and the experimental, between codes or freeform, refrain and abstract. Burnt on the alter of astonished and surreal communication, the music genres like rock, jazz, ambient and hip hop, lose their semantic meaning. No coded horizon does exist in the so called "Barnum of the *avant-garde*". Pussyfoot. Free from binding conditions. Free to be free. Irony as a liberating practice.

On the other hand, some antique civilizations did not believe, perhaps, that a cosmic laugh was at the origin of the world?

The Future.

"*Looking to the past is an act of exhaustion*", so say Elio Franzini and Maddalena Mazzocut-Mis in *Estetica*. In the microcosm of

Futuro.

"Rivolgersi al passato è un gesto di esaurimento" così Elio Franzini e Maddalena Mazzocut-Mis in "Estetica". Nel microcosmo Pussyfoot il passato è scomparso, non è fonte sonora a cui attingere. Semplicemente viene attivato, il passato, come sfondo, come testimonianza di un già esistente, come pre-testo. La tensione verso un universo futuribile è palpabile nelle loro proiezioni funky techno breakbeat. Gli artisti Pussyfoot non hanno scuola o *perìpatos* da seguire: tradizione e innovazione si alternano senza fine, in un universo caotico irriso e irrisolto, in una macchinazione divertente e visionaria. Da "gaia scienza" verrebbe da scrivere. Il loro estro futuribile ricorda da vicino il "cielo delle equazioni" di Velimir Chlebnikov o l'autocanzonamento dei cubofuturisti russi. La babele di singolarità fonetiche, musicali, artistiche ben si attagliano ad ambedue i gruppi: le acrobatiche dimensioni sonore di Howie B et alii sono simili alle smaglianti provocazioni dell'avanguardia russa guidata da Majakovskij. Infatti le irrequietudini artistiche sono simili in epoche che subiscono grandi trasformazioni sociali. Il binomio "futurismo-rivoluzione industriale" evolve, quindi, dialogicamente in "breakbeat-rivoluzione digitale". D'altronde non cantano sia il breakbeat che il futurismo, "la psicologia nuovissima del nottambulismo" metropolitano?

Ecologia dei suoni.

Parafrasando Deleuze, siamo così pieni di suoni che ce ne dobbiamo mondare. Non riusciamo più, infatti, a sentire un suono per quello che è realmente. In questa *megaphonia* dominante, il patchwork trasgressivo degli artisti Pussyfoot è quantomai parco e minimale, opera di una *Gestalt* creativa inusitata.
L'ordito ritmico, sbilenco e lacunoso, ritraccia il non udito.

Pussyfoot, the past has gone and it is no longer a sonic source from which to draw. The past is simply activated, as a background, as testimony to what already exists, as a pretext. The tension towards the future universe is palpable in their projection of the funky techno breakbeat. Pussyfoot, as well as its artists, do not have a school or a *peripatos* to follow: tradition and innovation alternate between themselves without an end, in a chaotic universe both derided and unsolved, in a fun, visionary scheme. A merry science universe, one would write. Their futuristic inspiration reminds from close up the "sky of equations" of Velimir Chlebinikov or the self-irony of the Russian *cubist-futuristic* artists. The chaos of the phonetic, musical and artistic singularity is well-suited to both groups, the acrobatic sound dimensions of Howie B are similar to the Russian avant-garde provocations driven by Majakovskij. In fact, artistic turmoil occur in times of great social transformations and are usually very similar. Therefore the binomial futurism-industrial revolution dialogically evolves into a breakbeat-digital revolution. But aren't they both (the Russian avant-garde and the Pussyfoot) perpetrating some ideals of the "Manifesto Futurista" such as the metropolitan "brand new psychology of the night life"?

Ecology of Sounds

Beginning by paraphrasing **Deleuze**, we are so full of sounds that we must try to peel away some of these. We are no longer able, in fact, to hear a sound for what it really is. In this dominant *megaphonia*, the outrageous patchwork of the Pussyfoot artists is minimal and parsimonious, an artwork from an uncommon, creative *Gestalt*. The rhythmic web, crooked and full of gaps, re-traces the unheard. The material fabric is a contemporary *merzbau* where the samples are delicate blend of propmen sounds and the track becomes, therefore, an explicit dadaistic sculpture. The sounds, selected

Toshio Nakanishi

Toshio Nakanishi

La tessitura materica è un *merzbau* contemporaneo dove i *samples* sono gracili frappe di *trovarobato* sonoro e le tracce sono quindi esplicite sculture dadaistiche. I suoni, scelti anche in base a una loro atipicità funzionale, trionfano nella loro purezza sporca ed elettronica. L'artista cerca intorno a sè le fonti sonore più disparate per rendere l'ascolto più innovativo e astratto possibile. Per ripetere l'incanto immacolato della prima volta, del primo ascolto, si enunciano differenze, si organizzano *metamatiche* e *metasoniche*, pur all'interno di una ripetitività ritmica per la pista da ballo. Una liberazione, ecco tutto: una schizofrenia visionaria di fonti audio, una itineranza delle asimmetrie, una ibridazione ironica di tempi e generi, una trasmutazione di blocchi di ambienti. Ecco cos'è la Pussyfoot di Howie B: un'anarchia felice, un caos elettronico ebete, un funk binario per i nuovi territori del suono nomade. Una teoria della liberazione attraverso una ecologia dei suoni. In altre parole, un vero e proprio manifesto per le nuove generazioni.

Ciak, si suona!

Più che dj, l'artista Pussyfoot è un *sound designer*. La generazione Pussyfoot è *cristallina* come direbbe Deleuze, scomposta com'è nell'*orecchio filmico*. Impregnata d'immagini fino al midollo, l'elettronica howiebizzante mastica una nuova grammatica, un coacervo di suoni che narrano anche *visivamente*, smarcandosi in modo logico e naturale dall'ossessività delle forme e del ritornello. Il procedimento artistico è all'opposto della colonna sonora. Qui sono le immagini interiori che hanno una loro sonorità, una loro ritmicità e che rimandano a territori inconsueti di densità significanti.

Il suono si organizza per spazi visivi, non più musicali. L'*inner cinema* dei vari World's End Girlfriend, Palmskin Productions, Spacer e Chari Chari è ben evidente in raccolte come **"Pussytoons"**, simbolico punto d'incontro tra il mondo del fumetto e quello del suono. Il fumetto non è altro che un luogo *esplosivo* di visioni e azzeramenti. *Un territorio esploso.* Nel fumetto ci si trova sbalzati in una macchina fantastica dove tutto è possibile. Da Mr. Magoo

ON THE WAY

HOWIE B.
MUSIC FOR BABIES

CRY

also for their atypical functional nature, triumph in their dirty electronic purity. The artist looks around to find the most disparate sounds to make the listening experience as innovative and abstract as possible. In order to repeat the immaculate experience of the first time, of the first listening, *metamatichal* and *metasonic* experiences are organised within a rhythmic repetition for the dance-floor. A liberation, a visionary schizophrenia of sonic styles, an itinerary of asymmetry, an ironic hybridisation of beat and genres. That's what Howie B's Pussyfoot is: a happy anarchy, an electronic chaos, a binary funk for the new territory of a nomad sound. A theory of liberation through the ecology of sounds. In other words, a true Manifesto for the new generation.

Ciak, play!

More than a DJ, the Pussyfoot artist is a *sound designer*. The Pussyfoot generation is *crystalline* as Deleuze would say, fragmented in the so called *film-ear*. Filled with images, Howie B's electronic, speaks a new grammar, an accumulation of sounds that narrates *also visually*, freeing itself logically and naturally from the obsession of the strophe and refrain. This artistic process is the opposite of the one of the soundtrack. Here the interior images have a proper sonority, rhythm and show a territory dense with meaning. The sound organizes itself based on visual space and not only on sound. The inside-cinema shown by various artists like World's End Girlfriend, Palmskin Productions, Spacer and Chari Chari is evident in collections like "Pussytoons", a symbolic meeting point between the world of comics and that of sound. A comic is nothing but an explosive place full of images and zero-settings. *An exploded territory.* In the comics we are thrown in a fantasy world where everything is possible. From Mr. Magoo to Doctor Spartaco, from Paperoga to Ranx Xerox, the *bande dessinèe* has created an imagery living in our childhood and beyond. The relationship between sounds and images defer to a new relationship between man and the world. Therefore, under the pretext of a sound

cover painting by Hubert Noi, art direction Toshio Nakanishi

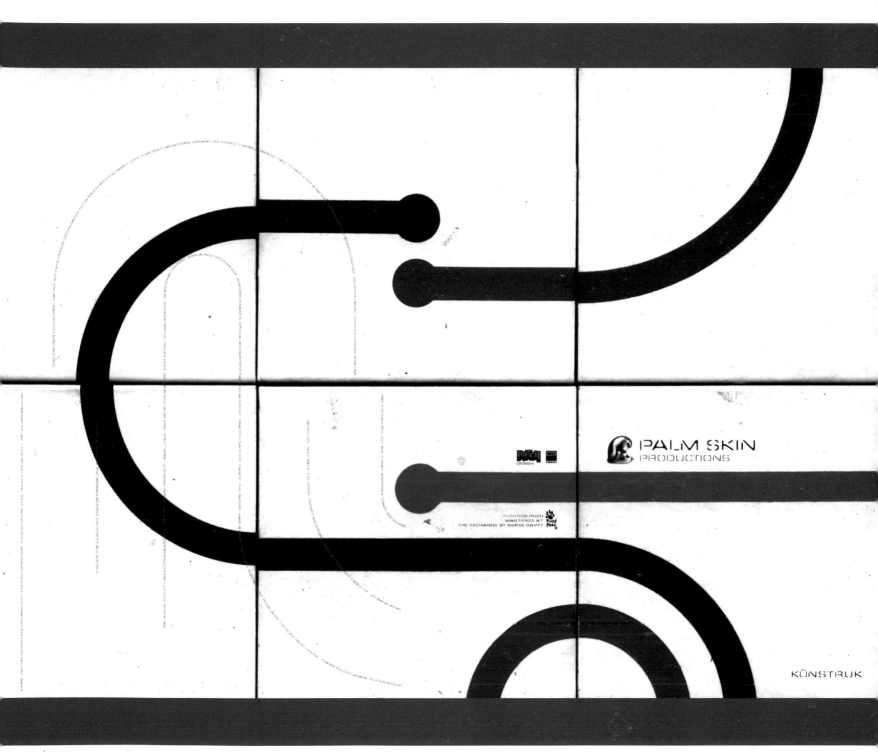

PALM SKIN
PRODUCTIONS

PUSSYCDLP010
MASTERED AT
THE EXCHANGE BY SIMON DAVEY

KÜNSTRUK

Mitch Design

al Dottor Spartaco, da Paperoga a Ranx Xerox, la *bande dessinèe* ha creato un immaginario che ha popolato la nostra infanzia. Il rapporto suono-immagine rimanda a un rinnovato rapporto *uomo-mondo*. Coesistono quindi nella finzione del *disegno sonoro*, le medesime armoniche fantastiche e i medesimi montaggi metalinguistici del *suono disegnato*, come in *Fantasia* di Walt Disney.

Il suono metaforizza l'interiorità delle esperienze. L'incrocio fecondo con il fumetto deflagra nell'irrompere dell'ironico, del giuocoso, del fantastico circense.

Paradigma artistico & alternative business.

Nel rivolgimento vertiginoso degli anni Novanta anche l'industria musicale mondiale è rimasta al palo. Sorpassata dalle tecnologie morbide delle autostrade informatiche, resa obsoleta dalla mobilità dei mercati e dei gusti, l'industria musicale stenta anche a reagire alla nuova figura paradigmatica portata avanti da artisti come Howie B. L'accento è posto dall'artista elettronico innanzitutto sulla libertà dalle costrizioni contrattualistiche, dal garantirsi l'integrità artistica, dalla liberazione del parossismo da classifica Top Ten, dalla manutenzione in proprio dell'immagine pubblica. Dotandosi di strumenti adeguati, cioè una propria etichetta indipendente, l'artista elettronico è vincente in quanto figura agile, ubiqua e dinamica nel relazionarsi sia alla scena artistica di riferimento, sia al mercato parcellizzato e di nicchia. Per le case discografiche *major* divenute "brand" di conglomerati industriali-mediatici assai ampi, l'esiguo margine di manovra sul *territorio* le ha rese patetiche balene bianche che sguazzano maldestre in un misero fiumiciattolo di montagna. *Small is beautiful:* ma questa è una guerra non combattuta, senza battaglie, senza veri vincitori, in quanto la soglia di sopravvivenza minima è sempre sfiorata, mai superata definitivamente.

Simbiosi grafiche.

La compenetrazione sempre più forte tra grafica, package e musica è un altro tratto distintivo dell'etichetta. Il *package*, non più modello di *design* con un mero scopo commerciale, diventa altresì *oggetto relazionante*. Le copertine di **Toshio Nakanishi** sono pura *simbiosi grafica* che dialoga con il contenuto sonoro dell'opera. Questa possibilità di dialogo

design, the same harmonic fantasy and the same meta-linguistic clips of the designed sound coexist, like in *Fantasia* by Walt Disney. The sound creates a metaphor based on the interior of the experience. The fertile intersection with the comics explodes in the ironic, playful, and fantastic Pussyfoot productions.

The artistic paradigm and alternative business

In the dizzy upheaval of the 90's, even the international music industry has remained at the post. Surpassed by soft-technology of the informatic highways, the music industry has difficulties in reacting to the new paradigmatic figure represented by artists such as Howie B. Here, the accent is given to the freedom from the typical contract constraints: from the guaranty of the artistic integrity to the maintenance of his own public image up to the freedom from the furious run to the Top Ten Classification. Giving himself adequate instruments, which means his own independent label, the electronic artist is a winning, agile and dynamic figure both for his reference point in the music scene and in the small, parcelled market of niche. For the big record company, more and more *majors* of large musical industrial conglomerates, the small margin for manoeuvre in which the same can operate reinforces the image of an enormous white whale wallowing in a dry stream... *Small is beautiful:* but this is an unfought war, without battles, without true winners, as the minimum survival threshold is always grazed, never clearly surpassed.

Graphic symbiosis

The ever-increasing connection between graphics, packaging and music is another distinctive aspect of the label. The packaging, no longer a model of design with only a commercial aim, also becomes a *relating object*. The covers of **Toshio Nakanishi** are examples of pure graphic symbiosis that dialogues with the content of the musical piece. This kind of aesthetic dialogue is very present and common in the Pussyfoot catalogue. The desired *wunderkammer* world of Snatch by Howie B, the tailcoat stromy-rocket of Bond in the Pussy Galore compilation, the abstract and child-like pictures of *Fish Smell like Cat*

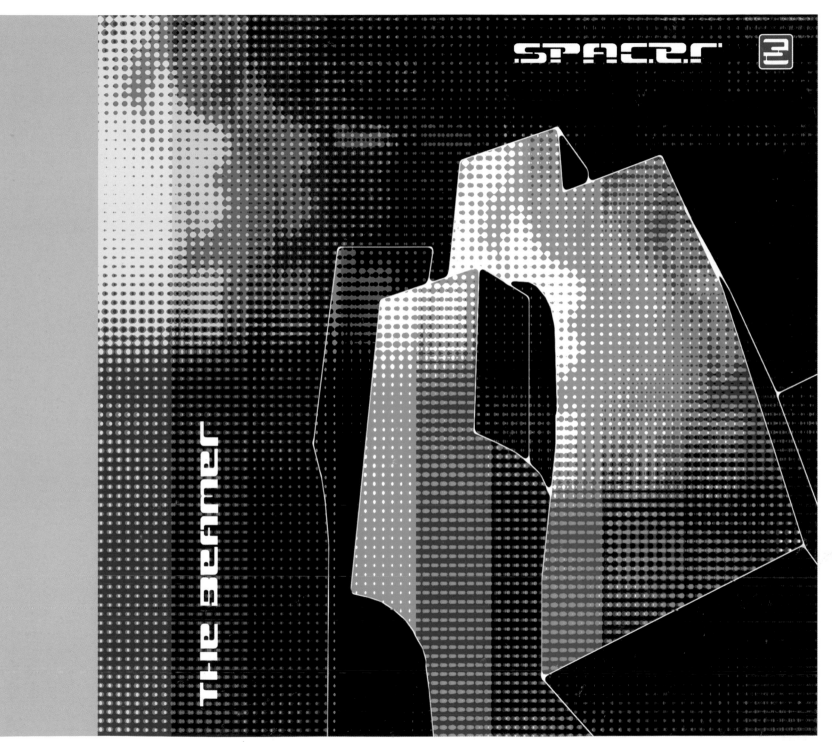

SPACER 3

THE BEAMER

Mitch Design

estetico è molto presente nel catalogo Pussyfoot. Il vagheggiato mondo *wunderkammer* di *Snatch* di Howie B, il *bufero-razzo* del Bond in frac nella raccolta *Pussy Galore*, le pittografie bambinesche e astratte di *Fish Smell Like Cat*, la grafolalia che invade le bambole adolescenti della raccolta *Suck It and See* mostrano un mondo analogamente speculare a quello sonoro. La percezione della simbiosi disegno-grafica-suono è totale. La comprensione dell'universo fantastico che sta *dentro* al disco è immediata. Pure l'artwork di **Mitch Design** per Spacer in *The Beamer* promuove la stessa sostanza: i monoliti informi, quasi *skyscrapers* asimmetrici vaganti nello spazio torvo, sono ingentiliti *a latere* da un viso di bambina sorridente che dà all'immagine di copertina un'altra lettura, meno tetra. Giuoco di specchi è quindi *The Beamer*, con l'immagine infantile posta in frammenti riflettenti, poliedrico rimodellamento della realtà oggettiva. E tale non appare anche il tech-funk futuribile di Spacer, così venato di allegra infanzia? E per finire, non è simile il geometrico *proun costruttivista à la* El Lissitzky della grafica di *Mitch Design*, con il rigoroso astrattismo breakbeat di **Palmskin Productions** in *Kunstruk*? Il *techno-cabaret* con ossessioni tedesche di Palmskin Productions sembra esprimersi anche nelle linee monocromatiche del tessuto grafico. La sua electro muta e satura di notte, da *metropolis* robotica, si riflette nei precetti comportamentali delineati all'interno dell'artwork: *fall to earth, get a tattoo, learn japanese, pay the gas bill, stop paying for sex, start recycling, make a living, get cable tv, go back home,* quasi fossero un abulico rosario di vacuità generazionale...

Sulla strada, dietro le quinte.

Tra sfolgorante giovinezza e "scienza-spettacolo", tra i grovigli della vita e il disarmo del sociale, nella piazza vuota coperta di foglie di pezza, l'artista Pussyfoot accenna a *motivetti* da ballo con il suo *laptop* portatile, giocoliere malinconico in tempi enigmatici e sospetti. La gioia per il giorno di festa appena trascorso potrebbe quindi finire qui, sulla strada, dietro le quinte del palcoscenico del mondo moderno.

Ascolti / Sounds:

Howie B – Snatch (Pussyfoot, Uk 1999)
Howie B – Music for babies (Polydor, Uk 1996)
Howie B + Sly & Robbie – Drum & bass strip to the bone (Palm Pictures, Uk 1998)
Spacer – The Beamer (Pussyfoot, Uk 2001)
Palmskin Productions – Kunstruk (Pussyfoot, Uk 2000)
Dobie – The sound of one hand clapping (Pussyfoot, Uk 1998)
Hal Willner – Whoops I'm an Indian (Pussyfoot, Uk 1998)
AA.VV. – Fish Smell Like Cat (Pussyfoot, Uk 1997)
AA.VV. – Pussytoons (Pussyfoot, Uk 2000)
AA.VV. – Pussy Galore (Pussyfoot, Uk 1996)
AA.VV. – Suck It and See (Pussyfoot, Uk 1998)

Letture / Words:

Elio Franzini – Maddalena Mazzocut Mis: "Estetica" (Bruno Mondadori, Milano 1996)
Angelo Maria Ripellino: "Saggi in forma di ballate" (Einaudi, Torino 1978)
Angelo Maria Ripellino: "Nel giallo dello schedario" (Cronopio, Napoli 2000)
Gilles Deleuze – Fèlix Guattari: "Millepiani. Capitalismo e schizofrenia. Sul ritornello" (Castelvecchi, Roma 1997) "Millepiani. Capitalismo e schizofrenia. Rizoma" (Castelvecchi, Roma 1997)
Ubaldo Nicola: "Atlante illustrato di Filosofia" (Demetra, Colognola VR 1999)
Gilles Deleuze: "L'immagine-tempo" (Ubulibri, Milano 1989)
Boccioni, Balla, Carrà, Russolo, Severini: "Manifesto dei Pittori Futuristi" (Milano, 1910)
Velimir Chlebnikov: "Poesie" (Einaudi, Torino 1968)

and the repetitive graphology that invades the adolescent dolls of the *Suck It and See* compilation, show an analogously specular world to the one of sound. The perception of the graphic-design-sound symbiosis is total. The understanding of the fantastic universe *inside* the record is immediate. Also the artwork of **Mitch Design** for Spacer in *The Beamer* supports the same content: the unshaped monolithic forms, almost asymmetrical skyscrapers, move through a darkened space but are at the same time refined by a child's smile giving to the image a less dark reading. *The Beamer* is then a mirror game, a polyhedral reshaping of the objective reality. And isn't the futuristic tech-funk of Spacer the same? So tinged with happy childhood? And again, isn't the geometric *noum costruttivista* à là El Lissitzky, from the graphics of Mitch Design, with the rigorous abstractionist breakbeat of **Palmskin Productions** in *Kunstruk* the same? The techno-cabaret with the German obsession of Palmskin Productions seems to express itself even in the monochromatic lines of its graphic design. Its dumb and nocturnal electro of a robotic metropolis, reflects itself in the behavioural precepts and rules written in the artwork: *fall to earth, get a tattoo, learn Japanese, pay the gas bill, stop paying for sex, start recycling, make a living, get cable TV, go back home,* almost as if it were an aboulic rosary of generational emptiness....

On the street, behind the fifth.

Between a blazing youth and a "science-show", between the tangle of life and the disarming of the social attitude, in an empty square covered in pieces of leaves, the Pussyfoot artist sketches some dance tunes with his portable laptop, as a melancholy juggler in enigmatic and suspect times. The joy of the merry day that has just passed could be finished here on the street at the backstage of the modern world.

an Wrake

Federino Ghiaia, cronista atomico di Grullopoli, ci rivela con il suo stile deragliante e sovraeccitato i misteri buffi del microcosmo sonoro Pussyfoot, etichetta dell'arcimaestro Howie B.
Talibano dell'elettronica masnada, Federino Ghiaia ci sciorina l'howiebismo, ironica scienza inesatta e pure tracotante.

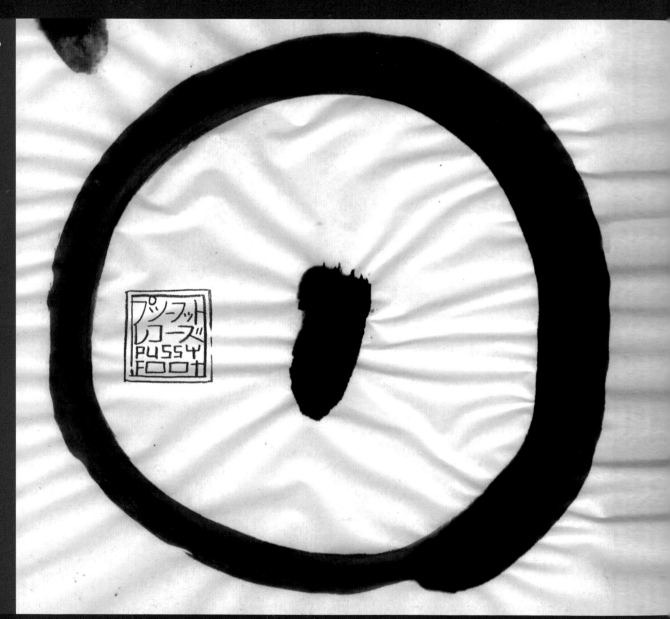

Toshio Nakanishi

FISH SMELL LIKE CAT
I nippopesci in esilio
nell'isola dei gatti

Disse Chuang-tzu: "Avete un grande albero e vi preoccupate della sua inutilità. Perché non lo piantate nel paese del nulla e dell'infinito?". Così la saggezza orientale del Tao. E se questo paese del nulla e dell'infinito avesse come capitale Elfonìa, città liquida e ingovernabile, còlma di suoni che dilagano senza forma, con melodie che s'inalberano ebbre, ritmi che franano nella polvere uno sull'altro e, nei rave sotterranei di cui la città è ghiotta, un pigiapigia di accordi taurini, note a brindello, arlecchinate rumorose, frastuoni, fischi e urla? E se questo paese del nulla e dell'infinito fosse abitato da seminatori di suoni quali il mago titano Howie B, gli uomini-gatto della Pussyfoot e i loro ittici bedlamiti sguazzanti nei mari del sole nascente? Le fanfare oniriche e festose di questo paese a Oriente di Arlecchino sono affastellate nell'adorabile operina **"Fish Smell Like Cat"** (Pussyfoot 05 - nov. 1997) che mette in mostra l'estro orecchiuto dell'Asia remota. L'almanacco giapponese che pubblica il signor Bernstein è, al solito, un delirio febbrile di **bits** fioriti e multicolori, di guitterie acidule e clownesche, di smèriglierìe esili e sintetiche, di ariette smilze da cat day afternoon.

Mirabile l'impegno, stupefacente il risultato, esterrefatto l'ascolto. Perché non cedere all'amorevole incanto di "Round &Round" di Tiphoon Tosh dove un lumacoso roccabilly, suonato ai 22 all'ora, è costruito su un basso polpetta, richiami d'uccello, una, falsa, Les Paul del '53 e una ramata di Moog? Mancano all'appello solamente: le verdure gratinate, una coppia di Ara Macao, il cugino californiano di Jonny Rockstar, la statua di Krucenich e il cerchio si chiude.

Eppoi di nuovo, prestate l'orecchio: ai meloni sonori dello shakeratore lunare tra tamburi tristi, pelli dei monti d'Atlante, bìsbiglii orientali e scatole di ritmi; alla nonchalance lisergica e arruffata di "She was beautiful"

di Ahh! Folly Jet, come a dire i Byrds che bighellonano sulla Via della Seta vestiti Comme des Garcons; oppure agli urinaux, i pappagalli, di Chari Chari con pìanti di gabbiani, smiagolìi, pentole di latta e melodie fatte di niente; da sfinire anche i più calmi poi, la poesia con le orecchie a sventola di "Snakes & Ladders" di Typhoon Tosh; qui la melodia pianta in asso il pezzo a metà, poi un violino con la mosca al naso s'inbizzarrisce, un fòlle inizia a declamare day became morning, morning became day quindi parte una girella psichedelica da California accattona con fidbacchi cipollini e trama desertica; il tutto, ineffabile, in una sola traccia. Ma che brodo di serpente ha sorseggiato questo tozzo di tifone...

Indimenticabile invece il quadretto dipinto da Girofreccia in "Mahalo Hotel", dove troviamo alla fonda samurai fischiettanti, lo zio scozzese di Howie B, forchette in marcia che mettono bacchette in fuga, scrosci di pioggia, sciòrinii di venti, letti sfatti, ritmi che pigliano a gabbo. "Ahh! Dimenticavo" argomenta l'arguto ascoltatore:"A che ora è la colazione?". "Non servono colazioni, al Mahalo Hotel. Per favore, lasci la stanza e paghi subito una grossa cifra!" sussurra a lui un Girofreccia sconsolato sotto la pioggia... Eeeh, ma che parapiglia in questo piccolo album giapponese! Gli altri miscidatori con le pinne a mandorla, i nippopesci del titolino sù in alto, smagriti puti in squame di tela non son da meno dei sopracitati. I softwaristi d'acqua salata di "Fish Smell Like Cat" ci offrono burle sonore eleganti, audioironie da isolani gracili e silenti, teneri dubbismi da folklore digitale e once di fantasia e bravura sparse a lisca di pesce. Ma Howie B, il re di questo Ottobre Musicale, dove ha snìdato questa corte straordinaria e vagabonda? Questo vitalismo a battuta dolce lo poteva trovare solo a Elfonìa, la liquida città, nel Cipango onirico che abita in noi...

Toshio Nakanishi

PUSSY GALORE   Howie Bond e l'operazione Spybreakbeat

Finita la Quaresima, la nidiata sfrenata di Hoxton Square, base segreta dell'operazione Spybreakbeat, si è rimessa al lavoro.

Capitanati dall'agente segreto Bond, **Howie Bond**, i nostri audioagenti capricciosi gettano alle ortiche il grigiore della routine inglese e incocciano in questa fantasiosa pantomima sonora di "Pussy Galore" (Pussyfoot CD 007 - Ott.1996). Il quaderno scombiccherato che gabella i falsi *Bond Theme* è soperchiamente consigliato sia ai cultori del vetusto spione albionico sia ai dogmatici folgorati dal trambusto del breakbeat. Alla squadra Pussyfoot non manca certo la fantasia e l'invito a pittare trafelati swing orchestrali, con al centro le mirabolanti corbellerie dell'ebete mascherato, si è quindi rivelato un ottimo copione da mettere in scena. Come al solito, quando la famiglia si riunisce, i convenuti superano sempre in numero ed estro i convocati. Ecco quindi presentarsi un chimerico dottore, un tal Zaius, espressionistico estensore di un assassinio con la seno-onda registrata nella città della scimmia. Oppure, sdoganati dal paese di Cuccagna, i fantasmatici Natural 7, maramei orientali in missione con "Secret of Natural 7". La gènia più assillata dal gagà in bombetta sembra quindi essere quella nipponica, non si capisce se per amor della baloccata o se per genuflessione alla reliquia occidentale. Infatti ecco sfilare la paonazza parata di personaggi a metà tra il reale e il fantastico, tra il serioso e la *pantalonade*: Typhoon Tosh, Major Force, Kensuke Shiina, Chari Chari, Toshio Nakanishi. Mancano all'appello il pro-zio giapponese di Howie B (che vivacchia al porto di Chiba), la sosia orientale di Lili Brik, il vigile urbano di Okinawa che elevò una multa ai Daddylonglegs tre anni fa e l'allegra brigata levantina è completa. Ed è proprio l'insolita coppia anglopponica di **Nakanishi & Bernstein** che propone l'unico reale tema bondesco, "Death of Fiona", un John Barry del 1965 che viene schizzato da un misterioso ordito di moog sonici e vaneggianti trottolii ritmici (per le melodie c'è sempre tempo!). Il rimanente lotto di tracce è fatto brillare dai manipolatori sonici della cellula Pussyfoot: tra i migliori doppiogiochisti, Spacer, naturalmente, con la sua orchestrata "Contrazoom". In conclusione, questa sarabanda golosa di palcoscenici spettatori e baldorie da subbuglio, ci regala una splendida recita musicale, unico tramite tra il falso mondo dorato della spia in frac e il contemporaneo mondo del breakbeat.

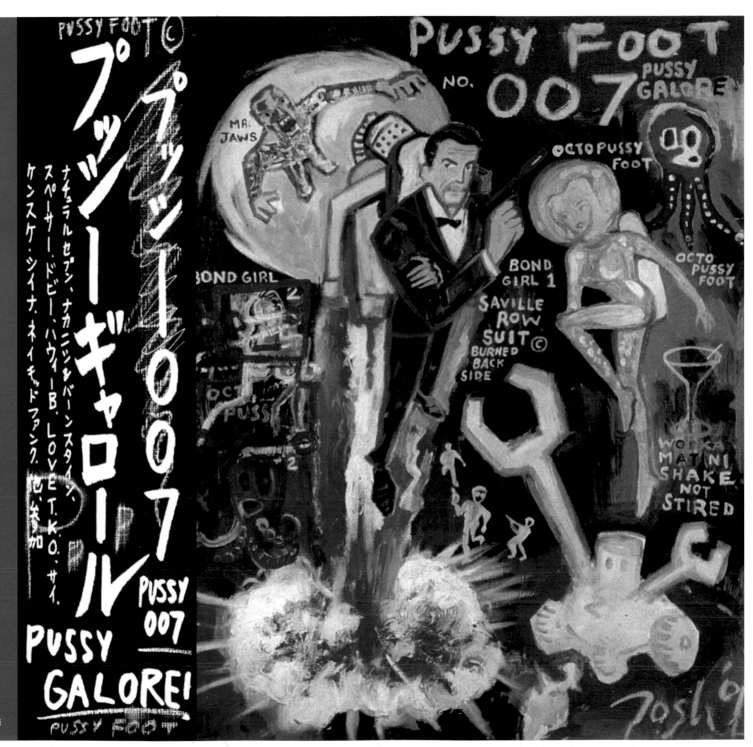

Toshio Nakanishi

SUCK IT AND SEE
Elogio della copula e delle cattive gioie della carne.

Non male l'ideuzza dell'ambient music per brache calate ("Suck it and see"- Pussyfoot CD069, Luglio 1998). "Succhia e vedi (cosa capita)" è l'ironico titolo dell'operina da lupanare escogitata dai malandrini della Pussyfoot. E certo tutti ci aspettavamo il gran successo riscontrato tra coloro ai quali fu demandato il pepato compito di musicarla: una cornucopia di brani, diciotto per la precisione, tanto da ingolfare due cd completi. Obiettivo primario: musicare roventi ingorghi sessuali, fatali ring amorosi, pornografici set di X-landia. Ringalluzziti dalle triviotematiche, i giramanopole di due continenti, Asia ed Europa, smanettano su maliziosi funk, sordide ballads e lascivi downtempo. Con ottimi risultati, non c'è che dire, per morigerati appicciccosi o educande dalla navigata moralità.

Così tra linguini e sospironi, ninfette ed ercoli da materasso, microdotati e *poupèe gonflables*, si snoda una frizzante, e innocua, *lingerie* sonora che darà fastidio ai più tediosi bacchettoni ma che mette di buon umore i più rilassati in materia sessuale. In ogni caso, siamo poco oltre Donna Summer e le sue gole profonde moroderiane. Vien in mente *aural sex*, ciarlando maliziosamente e con *pruderie* un pò da baraccone ma noi, giusto per stare al giuoco, apprezziamo assai questo breakbeat da luogo del malaffare. Perché, e chi ha memoria lunga lo ricorda, nacquero così, nel puttanesco serraglio degli slums più umili, molte delle musiche, e tra di esse il jazz dei primordi, che utilizziamo per le danze più sfrenate d'oggigiorno. Le cattive gioie della carne trovano così, anche in epoca asettica e digitale, meritato incastro, tra slip e breakbeat, tra camera da letto e pista da ballo. "This is my sex tape" ljubeggia la bionda *Lolita* manga disegnata da Toshio Nakanishi nel booklet interno. Perché non ascoltare? **Love** is the message!

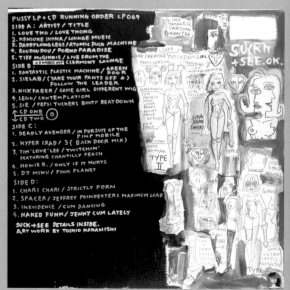

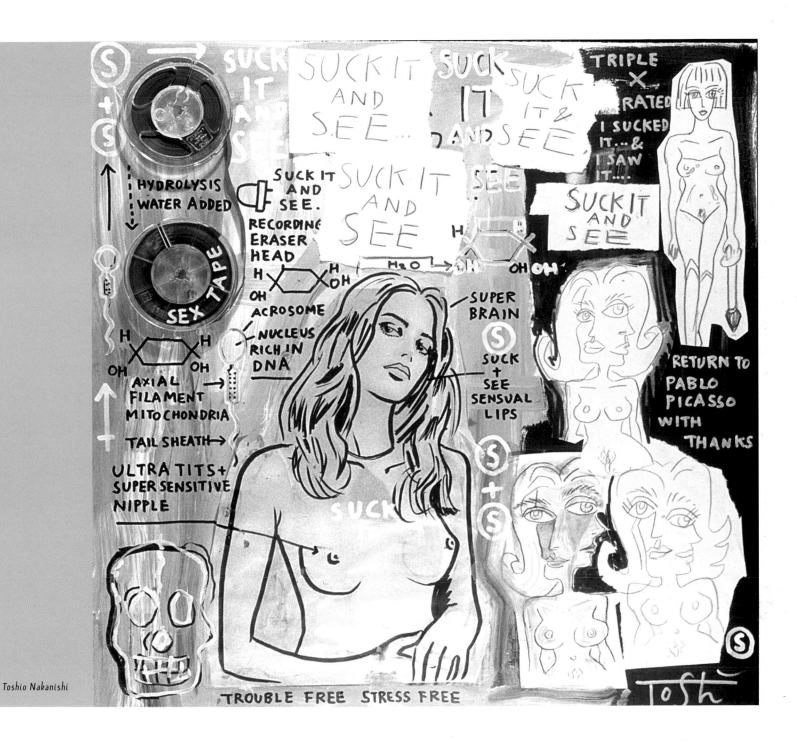

Toshio Nakanishi

MY LEFT FOOT
I guastatori sonici di casa Pussyfoot
sul piede (sinistro) di guerra

CD Cover (Japan version) by Toshio Nakanishi

La casamatta Pussyfoot chiama a raccolta I suoi ultimi dodici *zampini* per "My Left Pussyfoot" (Pussyfoot CD013, Maggio 1999). E qui **Howard Bernstein**, il Presidente del Globo Terrestre, tenta la formazione del Governo Mondiale del Breakbeat Scapigliato: un'epifania di americani, cinesi, giapponesi, due minatori gallesi, uno scozzese ubriaco, un serbo-croato, un babbuino, l'archimandrita di Gerusalemme e suo zio, Rodney Bernstein. Pare, anche la statua di Krucenich, ma non ne sono certo. La breakbeatnìa pseudoinglese parte con un *primer* del presidente dell'associazione dei 13 che ci ghirigora una nerbiosa poesia elettronica, "Five Days", a metà incrocio tra Snatch e Daddy Longlegs. L'insanìa prosegue balbettando un bel funk epilettico di Inevidence (Discodaze), uno spacejazz polveroso in orbita con una vecchia stazione spaziale sovietica di Deep Cops (Oi Diablo!), mentre Naked Funk ci rifila la solita barba assira con breaks e beats ciccioni e bzunt (Helium 3). Gli altri, più slombati, spargono magiche befane di pietra: **Sie downtempa**, elegante come sempre, in "Praying Mantis", **Adi Ludovac** (Put/Journey) iconeggia incerto tra i cubase, le cupole ortodosse e le voci bulgare, ma forse è il più in orbita di tutti. Le altre disordinate schegge reggono bene il martirio pussyfootiano: **Three Wheels Out** mostrano le loro vergogne adamitiche in "Under the road" (ma che ci faranno mai sotto la strada? Forse la manutenzione della serra sotterranea di funghi nel basement Pussyfoot?), **Minatone** violineggiano mentre la città dorme (The city sleeps), l'astronauta del breakbeat jungle Spacer ci mostra il suo libro mastro dove imbratta di suoni ciclopicamente metafisici "The Hollow Kick" (per inciso il brano migliore). Chiude l'almanacco il predicatore evangelico del breakbeat, Howie B. La sua "Freedom" è uno schizzo a battuta lenta tratteggiato con gran classe e maestria. L'eccentrica nidiata chiamata a raccolta da Mamma Gatta è una stregante tonsura dai più brumosi e defatiganti quotidiani. Vogliamo entrare nelle loro visioni e scrollarci di dosso le lugubri tartine pop che imbrogliano l'etere? Se sì, alcune risposte a questa domanda sono qui, iscritte nelle volute del suono, nei glissando elettronici, nei circuiti di silicio corrotti e dilatati. L'universo fantastico e il rifiuto ad integrarsi di questi sciamani del Breakbeat risulta rassicurante ed ammaliante per tutti noi.

Il mago-titano Bernstein ci sorride, il suo caravanserraglio di fantagatti dello spazio profondo ha colto nel segno. Gli angeli e i fantagatti, si sa, hanno la cocuzza pelata come Howie B.

'My Left Pussyfoot'

Kate Harrison

DADDYLONGLEGS

Colpo di scena in casa Bernstein! E' tornato papà!

Dietro a Daddy Longlegs, il *paparino gambelunghe*, si celano due breakheadz, i *doctores angelici* Howie B e Jeremy Shaw (una delle metà di Naked Funk), noti cavalieri della sorte sellata di stanza londinese. E' la loro prima corsa sulla lunga distanza dopo una frammentata e longeva disseminazione di piazzamenti in svariate *course de chevaux* in quota Pussyfoot, la compagine caotica di Howie B.
Riconosciamo subito al primo impatto, la macchina astratta, firma d'autore, dell'oracolo dei nuovi suoni, Howie B. Quando il piccolo scozzese è della partita, l'elettronica si fa concreta, spessa, quasi tattile.
I suoi materiali sonori, omogenei ed eterogenei allo stesso tempo, diventano flussi dove si mescolano rizomi solidi, grevi: c'è una densità dai colori mistici nella sua proposta che rifugge imperiosamente il già udito. I breaks transmentali del team Daddylonglegs, innervati di iperfunk, sono posseduti da una stralunata atipicità. I loro, sono breaks in divenire, quasi mai perfetti. Le anomalie infatti, vengono coltivate mai cancellate. Eclatante esempio di questa poetica è già la prima traccia equina, "*Pony Express*", dove la ciclopica sonata tecno-tribale non gareggia con le pavide robotracce, psichedelicamente analoghe, dell'ultimo album dei **Chemical Brothers**. Là dove i fratellini chimici ci confezionano un excursus finto-psichedelico trasparente, senz'anima, qui i **Longleggers** s'impolverano nella farina micologica, facendo leva sulla intelligenza corporea dei demonietti dediti al consumo illegale di breakbeat. Altro mirabolante esempio di *spirit dance* è il funk sporco e delirante di "*Giddy Up*" dove lo scollamento è clamoroso.

Il ritmo, pregno di groovismi da strada, caracolla alticcio e si trascina pittorescamente al galoppo per tutta la traccia. Sovraccarico, quasi dovesse portare una trave di carne addosso, "*Giddy Up*" incespica in un surplus di elettroniche primitive e polverose, diventando un esempio da manuale di funk sintetico e obliquo.
Lo straniante marginalismo astratto è rafforzato dall'abbecedario pop di "*When Betty Comes to Town*", una gracile bardatura sintetica, delicata fin nelle viscere e dove il canto e la chitarrina ne fanno un inusitato balbettio amoroso al chiaro di luna. La deflagrazione di elettronica subatomica continua nella cavalcata da dieci minuti di "*The Cobbler*", esempio funzionale di fantasia e creatività incalzante. Rimarchevole pure il mantello malinconico di "*Black Beauty*", strepitoso cammeo di immacolata intensità e il paranoico buco nero di "*They Shag Horses Don't They?*" dove un grezzo carillon elettronico di 303 innerva alla radice la traccia, saturandola con una densità auricolare tirata allo spasimo. La briglia neuro-funk si scioglie invece libera in "*Don't Milk Ya Hoss*", nerbioso brodo iperritmico dalle saettanti traiettorie, mentre l'ambient amniotica fa capolino nella embrionica bellezza di "*Bareback*". Chiudendo il salace mondo delle corse di Daddylonglegs, possiamo affermare che "*Horse*" (Pussyfoot CD016, Ottobre 1999) si fa amare per la foga funk aliena e liberatoria che scorazza a briglia sciolta per tutta la "pista" dell'album.
Che scuderia olimpica, quella di Howie B!!

Run Wrake

HORSE

Guggy

CLUB LIT

testi: Federico A. Amico
fotografie: Dario Lasagni

Cosa succede se nel club arriva la letteratura? Con tutta probabilità certi storceranno il naso ("aridatece il breakbeat!"), altri molto più semplicemente diserteranno la serata ("è un pacco!"), altri ancora non sapranno mai che la letteratura è entrata nei club. Ma perché mai dovrebbe farlo? Perché mai la letteratura dovrebbe varcare la soglia di uno spazio che non le è proprio? E soprattutto, chi è stato quello che gliel'ha permesso?

Discendono poi tutta un'altra serie di domande che ancora non sappiamo se in queste righe troveranno risposta, l'unico modo per scoprirlo è arrivare fino in fondo. Innanzitutto, sarebbe corretto azzerare la concezione della letteratura che tutti noi abbiamo mutuato dalle esperienze istituzionali legate a questa modalità espressiva. Dante, Boccaccio, Ariosto e poi Joyce, Musil, Svevo fino a Manganelli, Sanguineti, Perec ed Ellroy e tutto il resto della simpatica congrega degli scrittori, non solo hanno redatto parole, ma anche suoni, atmosfere, climi e mondi che sono stati relegati, per vizio ideologico, alla pagina stampata, trascurando che la loro sostanza possiede un aspetto sonoro assolutamente poco marginale. Quando poi, negli ultimi tempi e non solo, si è potuto costituire su basi solide il processo di "industrializzazione culturale", che ci ha inesorabilmente condotto alla pubblicazione di volumi a cura di pubblicisti, giornalisti, etc., abbiamo reciso ancor di più i legami profondi che la letteratura aveva stabilito con l'umanità. Così l'impressione che abbiamo oggi dei testi è intrinsecamente legata a luoghi quali la scuola, l'università, la biblioteca, le librerie, nei

CLUB LIT

text: Federico A. Amico
photo: Dario Lasagni

What happens if literature arrives in a club? Very likely, some will turn up their noses (give us back the breakbeat!) others will simply desert the evening (it is a cheat!!) still others will never know that literature entered the club. But why shouldn't one ever do this? Why should literature ever cross the threshold of a space that is not its own? And most importantly, who is the one who has allowed all this?? Another series of questions arise... but we still do not know if in these lines we will find a response to; after all the only way to discover it is to get to the bottom of the article.

First of all, it would be correct to zero the conception of literature as we have matured from the institutional experience connected to this expressive mode. Dante, Boccaccio, Ariosto and then Joyce, Musil, Svevo, Manganelli, Sanguineti, Perec, Ellroy and the rest of the pleasant group of writers, who have not only written words, but also sounds, environments, climates and worlds that we relegated, for ideological vices, only to the printed page, ignoring the fact that their substance possesses a sonorous aspect that is not very marginal. When, in the recent past, but not only, it has been possible to construct on a solid base the process of "cultural industrialization" that has inexorably conducted through the publication of volumes created by publicists, journalists, etc, we have cut off ever more the deep connections that literature had established with humanity. So, the impression we have today of texts is intrinsically linked to places like schools, universities, libraries, bookstores, in which, if you pay attention, we usually

quali, se ci fate caso, di solito ci troviamo a sussurrare, quasi a testimoniare che la pronuncia delle parole sia un'attitudine pressoché delittuosa.

Ma se io scrivo sulla pagina delle parole è anche perché queste possono essere pronunciate, dette, nella mia inflessione, con i miei accenti, possono insomma portare nel loro profilo anche altri elementi capaci di chiarificare/testimoniare ulteriormente il significato che ad esse voglio dare nel disporle, utilizzarle, sceglierle. Quando poi si profila all'orizzonte tutta una genia di scrittori quali **Irvine Welsh, Tiziano Scarpa, Aldo Nove, Alan Warner**, e molti altri ancora, il cui registro tende a rielaborare l'inflessione della strada, ci viene il dubbio che il libro, la pagina stampata, non sia uno strumento autosufficiente, un oggetto capace di racchiudere nei propri limiti fisici la loro parola.

Solitamente e storicamente sono stati i teatri i luoghi in cui la parola ha preso corpo, attraverso l'opera dell'attore e del regista, ma progressivamente le platee si sono fatte deserte e gli stessi autori si sono trovati costretti a rinunciare al confronto con tale mezzo. Senza dimenticare che regista e attore conducono sul testo una *interpretazione*, la quale sicuramente accresce il valore dell'opera, aggiungendo ad essa *inediti aspetti*, ma l'inflessione dell'autore continua ad essere assente, latitante.

Con i teatri vuoti, con i libri rinchiusi negli scaffali delle biblioteche e librerie, insomma in un panorama assai paludato e stantio, le istanze primarie di chi non vuole interrompere la propria ricerca e contemplare anche l'attitudine orale del proprio fare scrittura trovano quale luogo naturale attraverso cui far emergere la totalità della propria esperienza probabilmente proprio il club. Anche perché è attraverso questo luogo che tutto un mondo ha saputo riaggregarsi nel nome della ricerca musicale, superando di slancio tutti gli ostacoli che un mondo governato dalla produttività imponeva.

whisper, as to testimony that the pronunciation and the utterance of the words is a habit nearly criminal. But if I write words on the page, it is also because these can be pronounced, said, with my inflexion, with my accent and they can carry other elements capable of clarifying or witnessing the final meaning that I want to place, choose or use. Then, when one profiles an entire group of authors, which includes Irvine Welsh, Tiziano Scarpa, Aldo Nove, Alan Warner and still many others, whose tune tends to re-elaborate the inflection and the vivid expressions of the language of the street, we begin to doubt that the book, the printed page, isn't a self-sufficient instrument , an object capable of closing in its physical limits the power of the words.

Historically theatres have been places where words have taken form through the work of an actor and the director, but progressively the stalls have been deserted and the same authors have found themselves forced to give up this type of performance. Without forgetting that the actor and director conduct an interpretation of the text which surely increases the value of the piece, adding certain aspects. With empty theatres, with books put back on the shelves of libraries or bookstores and in such a stale panorama those who do not want to interrupt their own research and want to contemplate the experience of a language performance, can do it in a club. Also because it is through this place that a great many people in the name of musical research have passed and overcome all obstacles imposed by a commercial world governed by productivity. If then one turns to a club and its corridors to describe the evolution and social involvement that are represented inside, both literature and the club-culture do not find themselves representative of two worlds radically separated one from the other but instead of two perfectly penetrating.

Se poi ci si rivolge al club e ai suoi corollari per descrivere le evoluzioni e involuzioni sociali che ci stanno attorno, la letteratura e il club non si trovano più rappresentare mondi radicalmente separati l'uno dall'altro, ma si compenetrano ottimamente.

Il cut-up, la tecnica che con **William Burroughs** ha ridisegnato la modalità espressiva di innumeri scrittori, non è forse assai simile alle modalità compositive che il breakbeat ha saputo proporre negli ultimi anni? Ricostruire una narrazione attraverso il taglia e cuci delle parole non è forse una chiara esemplificazione del procedimento che tutti i produttori di musica elettronica stanno attualmente utilizzando per infiammare le piste di tutti i club d'Europa? Perché allora la letteratura deve rimanere costantemente relegata a pratiche di fruizione che la costringono al silenzio? Non può essa interagire con un pubblico? Non può recuperare le sue funzioni di innovazione espressiva attraverso una performatività dell'autore stesso, che è così costretto a mettere in gioco tutto il suo fare: il tracciare i profili delle parole, assegnare ad esse un significato, pronunciarle secondo i propri intenti, fletterle alla materialità del suono?

E' forse per rispondere a queste esigenze che ha preso corpo **ClubLit**. Gli interpellati sono stati invitati sul palco perché la propria opera assumesse una forma sonora che altrimenti sarebbe sfuggita o rimasta potenziale. Portare degli autori in un club vuole quindi essere tutto questo e altro ancora. La musica e la letteratura sono sicuramente le due forme espressive primigenie che, assieme alla pittura, hanno accompagnato l'uomo lungo tutta la sua storia. Se siamo pronti ad apprezzare quanto di meglio i breaks e i bit dell'ultima ora propongono, dovremmo essere in grado anche di affrontare la parola scritta o detta che sia, nel tentativo di recuperare un rapporto con essa che trascuri finalmente gli appellativi che ci hanno insegnato a utilizzare (mattone, pacco, palla) e che, di nuovo per vizio ideologico, ci hanno tenuti separati da un mondo fantastico come quello rappresentato da questo tipo di espressione. Senza dimenticare che attraverso la parola possiamo ridere, piangere, stupirci, ovvero ripercorrere tutta una gamma di emozioni, tanto quanto questo avviene attraverso la musica, e il suono sintetico o organico che noi produciamo è semplicemente una variante della parola, anch'essa musica, anch'essa melodia. Non so se tutto questo sproloquio abbia risposto esaurientemente alle domande che abbiamo posto inizialmente, sicuramente si potrebbe aggiungere ancora molto, ma lo spazio è tiranno, per cui, dato che siamo delle carogne, poniamo un ulteriore quesito.

Se la musica elettronica conduce una ricerca tesa alla sintesi di anima ed esattezza attraverso il dancefloor, la rappresentazione performativa della letteratura può assolvere, secondo i canoni suoi propri, allo stesso compito?

ClubLit è nato all'interno della prima edizione di Clubspotting per poi diventare una rassegna che si è tenuta al Maffia nella stagione 2000/2001 e che ha visto partecipare: Raul Montanari, Aldo Nove, Tiziano Scarpa, Arturo Bertoldi, Giuseppe Caliceti, Andrea Canova, Stefano Raspini, Rosaria LoRusso, Lello Voce, Isabella Santacroce e il collettivo Baobab.

Le serate in questione sono state rese udibili sul sito: www.clublit.it.

The cut up, the technique through which William Burroughs has redesigned the expressive mode of innumerable writers isn't in some way similar to the compositive way that breakbeat has proposed in the last years? Reconstructing a narration through the cut-up of the words is perhaps the clearest example of the process which the producers of electronic music are actually using to fire the dance-floors of all the clubs of Europe. Why then must literature remain constantly relegated to a fruition that induces silence? Can't it interact with the audience? Can't it recover its function of expressive innovation through a performance of the author, who is then forced to put everything into his/her act: the profile of the words, assigning meaning, pronouncing his or her own intentions, bending the content to the materiality of the sound? It is perhaps in response to these needs that ClubLit has taken form during this season at the Maffia Club. The authors had been invited to perform on the stage so that their show or reading could assume a sound form that otherwise would have been just potential. Introducing literary authors in a club means all of this and still more.

Music and literature are surely two primitive expressive forms, which together with painting have accompanied man throughout his history. If we are ready to embrace the latest and great breaks and bits recently proposed, we must be able as well to face the written or spoken word for what it is, in the attempt to recover a relationship with something that neglects the appellatives which we have been taught to use (cheat, bore, drag...) and again that ideological vice, which has kept us far from a fantastic world such as the one of the literature. Also we cannot forget that through words we can laugh, cry, surprise, or run a wide range of emotions, exactly as it happens with music, and that the synthetic or organic sound that we produce is simply a variant of words, and easily can be read as a music, a melody.

I don't know if all this talk has responded sufficiently to the questions we posed at the beginning; surely one could add still more, but the space is tyrannical. So, knowing we are skunks, we propose other quests. If, through the dance floor, the electronic music conducts a research turned out to synthesise the soul and the exactness of its expression, can the performance represented by literature absolve, according to its own canon, the same work?

ClubLit is a review held at the Maffia Club in the season 2000/2001 and that has seen the participation of: Raul Montanari, Alde Nove, Tiziano Scarpa, Arturo Bertoldi, Giuseppi Caliceti, Andrea Canova, Stefano Raspini, Rosaria LoRusso, Lello Voce, Isabella Santacroce and the collective Baobab.

The evenings in question can be heard on the site: www.clublit.it

DELTA FUTURA MODE2 AT A CLUB CALLED **MORe**

A project made in

SARTORIA
comunicazione

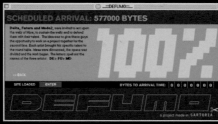

 DELTA FUTURA MODE2 AT A CLUB CALLED **MORe**

Welcome to Defumo.org! DElta, FUtura and MOde2, that is. For some of you out there, these artists need no presentation at all. Others might not know. Whatever the case might be, we hope you'll find this project interesting enough to be worth its heavy load. It all started in Modena, Italy, around spring in 2000: in a club called MORe, Delta Futura and Mode2 joined forces to create a unique piece of art out of the walls of the venue. Sartoria propelled the whole thing into being and made sure cameras was rolling at all times. Mo' Wax provided the soundtrack.

SlamJam supported the project. Defumo.org presents you with plenty of images, sound, animation,video,interview clips (make sure you check DEFUMO TALKS). A limited edition DVD package is in the making. More features will be added to this site, so stay tuned and most of all...enjoy it.

Three Giants from the Write-side:
Delta (Amsterdam), Futura (NYC), Mode2 (London/Paris).

Destination: an unlikely stomping ground.
Europe/ Northern Italy/ Province of Emilia Romagna/
Town of Modena/ Via del Lancillotto.
A club named More.

Here's how the project called DEFUMO took form and why.

1985: A section of a community sports center is transformed into a cultural happening, Graffio.
Several of its members are now part of the Sartoria.com crew. Graffio's musical, theatrical
and cultural program sets a new standard for clubs in Emilia Romagna and Northern Italy.

Graffio becomes Nine with a new crew of people who frequented Graffio. Nine then becomes
More offering dynamic musical programming coupled with internet facilities in the main room.
DJ sets and live performances Rainer Truby , DJ Vadim, James Lavelle, the Arsonist

The walls of More are its archives, its family album: there are layers of graffiti and paint that
testify to those who passed through this space and lived within it. The Solution is mathematical.
If the threat is to subtract something precious from a community, act by adding. How better
to conserve the walls of More, of Nine, of Graffio, than
by adding a new layer?

Delta, Futura and Mode2, were invited to act upon the walls of More; to sustain the walls
and to defend them with their talent. The idea was to give these guys the opportunity to
work on a project together for the second time. Each artist brought his specific talent to the
round table. Ideas were discussed, the space was divided and the work began. The letters
spell out the names of the three artists: DE> FU> MO

▶ MODE2

▶ MODE2

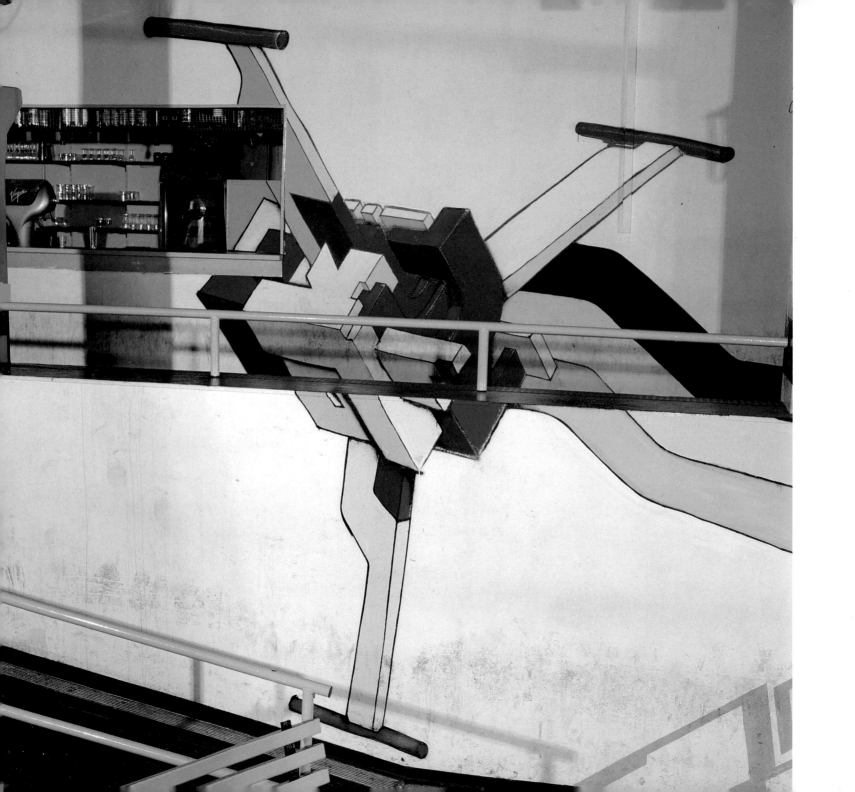

I LIKE BASIC COLOURS, I LIKE TO FOCUS ON
SHAPE, AND COLOURS CAN HELP EXPLAIN THE
SHAPE SO THAT WORKS BEST WITH BASIC
STRONG COLOURS.
Delta_

WELL MODE IS INTO FIGURES AND ALSO GRAPHIC
SHAPES. I THINK WHEN WE WORK TOGETHER IT
COMBINES VERY MUCH BECAUSE I THINK WE
ARE VERY MUCH OPPOSITES, I DON'T KNOW FOR
SURE BUT THATS HOW I FEEL, THE THINGS HE
DOES ARE VERY WARM AND SOULFUL.
_Delta

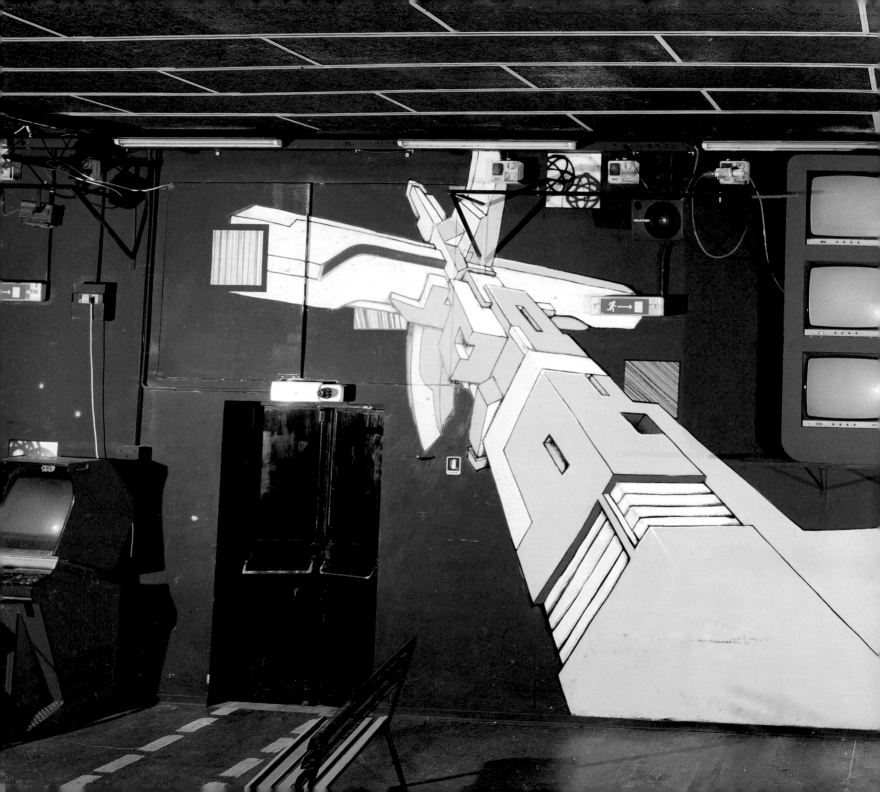

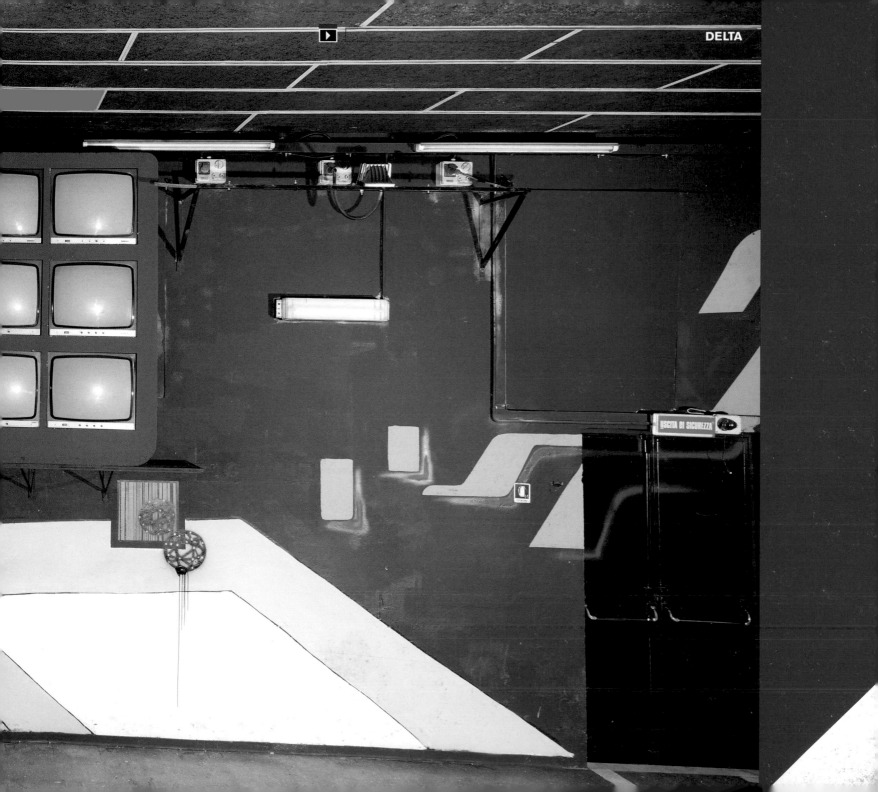

DELTA

▶ **FUTURA**

WELL WHEN I LOOK AT FUTURA FOR INSTANCE,
WHEN I LOOK AT HIS WORK, IT LOOKS REALLY
WELL, SO IT PUTS A LOT OF PRESSURE ON ME. I
AM LUCKY THAT I AM NOT IN THE SAME KIND
TERRITORY AS HE IS, OTHERWISE I WOULD BE
PARALIZED TO DO ANYTHING.
_Delta

▶ **FUTURA**

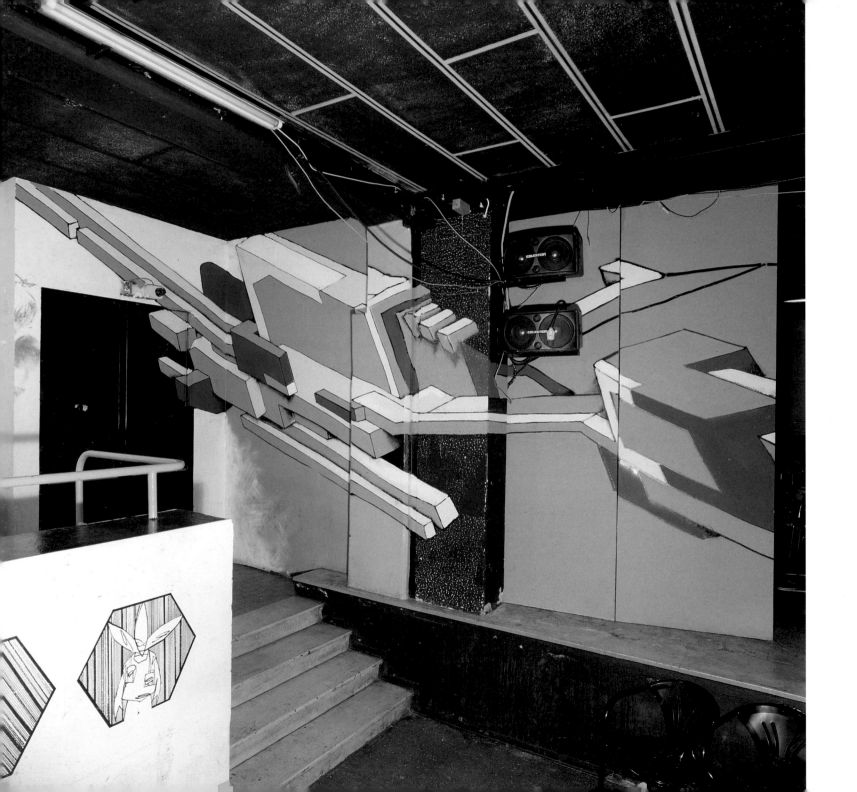

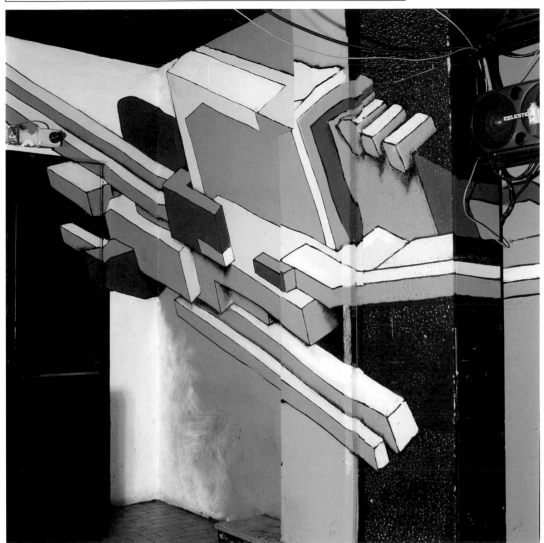

MOST OF THE TIMES ITS BETTER TO JUST START
WITH JUST A LITTLE BIT OF PLAN INSTEAD OF
MESSING EVERTHING ELSE UP BEFORE, 'CAUSE
I LIKE IT WHEN IT JUST HAPPENS.
_Delta

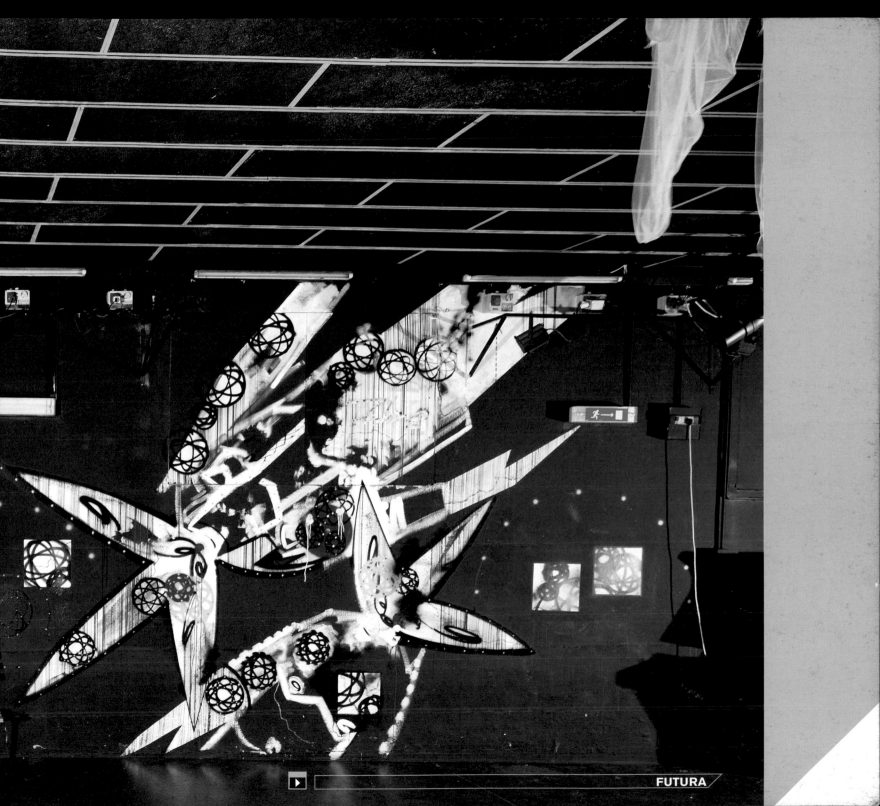

SOMETIMES I AM AREOSOL ONLY, WHICH IS JUST WITH A CAN, SOMETIMES I AM ACRYLIC PAINT WITH A BRUSH, AND OTHER TIMES I DOING WHAT I CALL GRAPHIC WORK LIKE ILLUSTRATION OF CHARACTER SOMETHING LIKE THIS SO IN THIS WAY. IN THIS JOB I WANT TO SHOW ALL OF THOSE THREE ELEMENTS SO IN FACT ITS A MAP OF MY STUFF.
_Futura

FUTURA

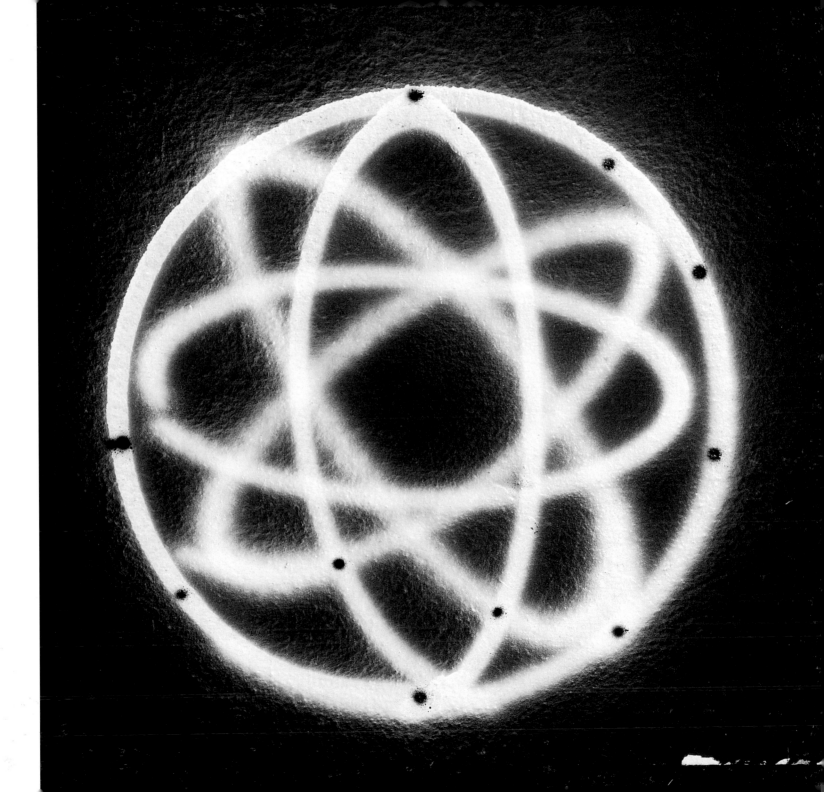

I LIKE COLOR IN COLOR

FUTURA 2000

LAUNCH JPEG
FUTURA 2000 SQUARES
LAUNCH VIDEO

- HIGH BAND
- LOW BAND

AND DON'T FORGET TO VISIT
WWW.FUTURA2000.COM

FUTURA 2000 EXAGONS
MARKER ON WALL

7 86936-0160-5

 FUTURA

LENNY IS VERY CHAOTIC. THIS DISCUSSION ME
AND BORIS HAVE, ABOUT WHERE'S THE
GENIUS IN LENNY, WHETHER EXPERIENCE,
TECHNIQUE, OR INSTINCT. ANYONE CAN SPLASH
PAINT AROUND BUT THERE'S SOMETHING ABOUT
THE GESTURAL THAT'S JUST HOW IT SHOULD BE,
YOU CAN'T IMAGINE IT ANYWAY AFTER THAT.
_Mode

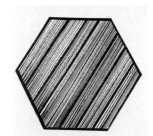

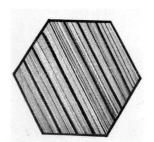

COLOR IS VERY IMPORTANT BUT THE MIXTURE OF
COLOR IS DANGEROUS. I LIKE COLOR IN COLOR,
AND ITS OWN SENSE OF COLOR, MEANING I LIKE
TO MORE OR LESS LIMITATE COLOR WITHIN THE
BARRIER OF ITS COLOR WITH A LITTLE ACCENT OF
ANOTHER COLOR TO MAKE IT CONTRAST. BUT I AM
INTO MONOTONE STYLE OF COLOR, I LIKE THE
CONTINUITY, UNIFORMITY, JUST THE COMPLECTION
OF A COLOR BECAUSE IT BECOMES MORE PURE.
_Futura

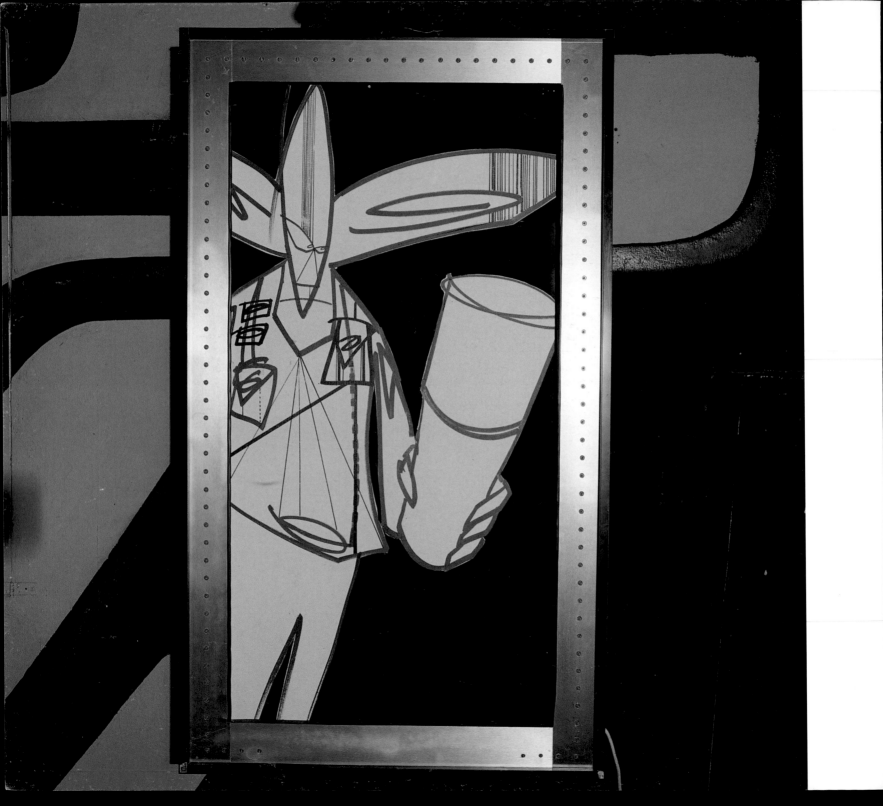

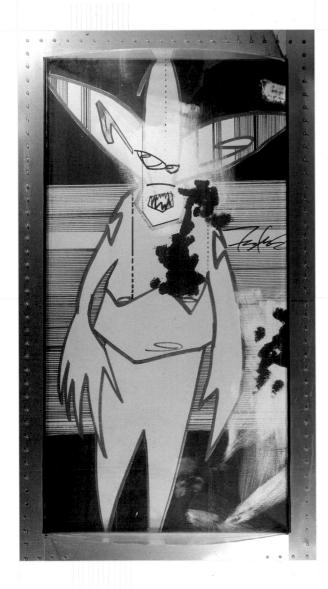

MY STYLE IS THAT I HAVE NO STYLE. MY STYLE IS
TO BE DETERMINED. MY STYLE WILL BE
DISCOVERED WHEN THE MOMENT HAPPENS
BECAUSE WHAT I AM GOING TO PAINT HERE
WILL EFFECT WHAT I AM GOING TO PAINT
EVENTUALLY THERE.
_Futura

FUTURA

BORIS IS SOMEONE THAT I MET THROUGH
SHOE, THE AMSTERDAM CONNECTION BACK IN
'86. HE LITERALY APPLIED 3D TO LETTERS.
LOADS OF PEOPLE HAVE TRIED TO COPY IT BUT
NONE CAN ACTUALLY, THEY GET TOO ANALYTICAL
SO ITS LIKE BEATING AN EGGWHITE TO LONG
AND IT BECOMES FLAT.
_Mode

WE EACH HAVE TOTALLY DIFFERENT STYLE, TECHNIQUE, AND APPROACH TO A JOB. THESE GUYS ARE MORE MENTALLY ORGANIZED OKAY, THEIR PREPARATION IS MORE EXACT. ALL OF US HAVE OUR CERTAIN APPROACH TO WHAT WE DO. LIKE I SAY, ME ITS JUST MORE SPONTANEOUS.
_Futura

AS SOON AS YOUR NOT DOING SOMETHING
ILLEGAL SOMEWHERE YOUR NOT WRITING. IF YOUR
NOT TRYING TO WORK SOMEWHERE YOUR NOT
WRITING.
_Mode

MODE2

DELTA

DELTA FUTURA MODE2 AT A CLUB CALLED **MORe**

"Are you down for this project with Lenny and me in Italy?
Painting in some club, no pay, but we get fed, and I mean fed!" knowing Mode, this could be interesting.
So I went there not actually knowing whatfore, besides that the company and the food was good.
Only after a couple of days/diners later I started to understand what this project was about; preserving the good ole more club by uplifting it and make something special happen.
A statement for the city, but also for the movement.

The three of us did a project together the year before; painting walls and surroundings for a dance-music festival in Paris. Very nice project aswell. That is where we met Giorgio and where he got the idea of organising the More-experience. We found out that planning and mapping out the walls beforehand was not the best way to do it. With this crew it is better to have some loose sketches and just see what happens on the spot. It is kind of a awkard feeling walking into the venue in the beginning, knowing that in a week we will have painted everything, but you do not have a clue how it will look in the end. I am very proud and honoured of the end result. It is always very inspiring to work with Mode and Futura. And lots of new ideas come to through working together.

That, combined with the hospitality of Giorgio and the Sartoria and the More crew, wait I am forgetting Massimo, Lara and the Osteria Francescana, ...hey G, let's do it again...
Cheers,

Boris

FUTURA

DELTA FUTURA MODE2 AT A CLUB CALLED MORe

it is rare for me to consider collaborations in spraypainting. unless of course a project would involve Mode2 and or Delta. as friends and respected artists from our culture, I am honored to work with them.

We have previously done projects together and the possibility of going to Modena, home of good friend Giorgio and Ferrari, was very exciting.

The plan was to paint a club called MORe, take part in a documented event and eat like kings (grazie Massimo).

What did evolve was a work in progress/think tank, that allowed us to use our specific technical abilitiesin a unity of color and design.

Creatively this project has gone beyond anything I could have imagined.
In that the actual work we did grow from discussion and energies shared during the moment.
Was this motivated by excellent food and drink?

The aftereffect expands to the web with the creation of www.defumo.org and other visual packages.
for me DEFUMO is a rare happening stimulated by friendship and understanding. our part is in credit to all the other players who made it a delight to create for fun&food .

                                                                    Futura

MODE

DELTA FUTURA MODE2 AT A CLUB CALLED **MORe**

In 1998, at a festival called "GLOBAL TEKNO" in Paris, Delta, Futura, and myself had decorated a large portion of the "Grande Halle de La Villette". We painted the hoardings that had been fixed into place to differenciate each particular performance area, and we set ourselves the task of giving the public a sense of direction and orientation through the site, as well as entertaining and stimulating them visually.

Once the show finished, and Futura and Delta gone back to their respective cities, it was left to me to take the last pictures of everything we had done, before destroying them all with a couple of cans of paint and a fatcap. We had no place to store them and, as they were easily detachable, we did not wish to leave them for anyone else to have.

In february 2000, I was working at Sartoria in Modena, and happened to end up at the "More" club one friday night. Giorgio explained to me the history of the club and, with Deemo, the different paintings on the walls and their origins were explained to me.

As Giorgio had already met Delta and myself through Futura, on the decor of "Global Tekno", an idea sparked in my mind that we could perhaps redo the experiment, but in a more intimate and permanent fashion than previously; at "More" itself. Giorgio, aware of the potential of such a project, then set the whole machine going, trusting our capacities, believing in the idea, and stretching and developing it into that magical week spent in Modena in april 2000.

Although we had worked together before, what the "DEFUMO" project became was something quite singular in all my painting experience. De, Fu, and myself were together in Modena for the first time, feasting at La Francescana, powered by the panini of Bar Schiavoni for our lunch hour, and consequently exploring more than just painting freely with different media; read FOOD. We discussed and debated over the food we ate, even cracking jokes about walking round Modena with "WILL WORK FOR FOOD" signs dangling from our necks. It felt, and tasted, so good and was so inspiring to meet "artists" and craftsmen who were at least as passionate about what they did as we were; and even then the food was not the end of the story!

We met Enzo Ragazzini, who was to take the pictures of the finished work, and his brother Paolo, and then there was some other crew from Milan with Colombo and Seba. Claudia was catching precious moments on DV, as she filmed the whole development of the "work", and the Sartoria crew had our backs.

Music was always pumping in the background, whether "Two Pages", "Trip Tease", "New Forms", or the "Anokha" compilation from me, Delta's own CDs, and what MP3's Futura managed to dig up on his "Bronze" Powerbook, before a bottle of beer spilled over it and spelt an end for such extravagance.The Slam Jam crew from Ferrara presented us each with a "little" bag full of wearable goodies, and even Fraser Cooke and his then-girlfriend Ai passed through, and more revelry was had around dinner-table with new-found friends.

At the "More" Giordano and his crew took care of all the trimmings, and came through with the smokables when we had no time to roll our own. The tempo of the week was set by all of these factors, and we allowed them to shape and to readjust what we had originally planned; the sketches and ideas let themselves be shaped by all those passing moments.

Further musical stimulus came as a donation from James Lavelle for the DVD, and the work of the Sartoria team in marrying the footage to the music was remarkable; "amazing" as Giorgio would say! I don't think anyone laughed more at the first cut of the DVD as Delta, Futura, and myself, as all the souvenirs came directly back.

I cannot really talk about the painting itself, as the act of painting is very hard to put into words; it is just something you do. You can look at the pictures taken of DEFUMO by Enzo Ragazzini when they will be up at the exhibition, you can look it up on www.defumo.org, or wait to catch the finished DVD, if you're really lucky; but nothing replaces the actual act of painting, the actual process of execution. Strangely enough, the act of drawing or painting is a process through which I inadvertently distance myself from the vision or statement that I bring forth, as if it is expelled once and for all from my being.

I have absolutely no pretention of being a "créateur" of any kind. That is either the task of what some call God, or the act of a woman and a man creating a child. Furthermore, however close the creative process may seem to compare itself to the act of "giving birth" to an idea or a vision of some sort, I am only a man and cannot be a substitute to woman and that true power which is hers only. We only translate into a form of visual dialogue what we have in our heads and what our spirit dictates.

I see DEFUMO as an opportunity offered to De, Fu, and myself to explore our ideas, potential, and capacities of interacting harmoniously together while exploring personal horizons, an opportunity to write some kind of contemporay piece of music for a trio of multi-instrumentalists. The opportunity to use the paintbrush, spraypaint, the pencil, the marker, projecting from black and white digital files, negative photos, or from direct fibre-tip pen drawing on acetate; DEFUMO provided a chance to explore all these visual avenues.

We had got away from the "Graffiti-job" briefs and were free to use whatever seemed more aesthetic, harmonious, appropriate, or practical for what we, as individuals wanted to do in this group piece. It was a chance to make short-sighted clients understand, once and for all hopefully, that we are craftsmen with vision and ideas, and not limited solely to the clichés that they have already earmarked for us.

I do not expect them to know anything about the actual importance of our culture in contemporary graphic, art, and social history, but at least to be honestly curious and less presumptually condescending about the part we have played in shaping today's graphic environment.

It's incredible what efforts have been put in by so many for a project as gratuitous as this, as no everyone did their bit for free. I really felt that this was just for the hell of it.
One word of warning though; watch out for the parcita....it could be dangerous.

Mode

DELTA FUTURA MODE2 AT A CLUB CALLED **MORe**

SARTORIA would like to acknowledge the following for their efforts:

First and foremost the artists: DELTA, FUTURA and MODE2
Everyone at club MORE, in Modena.
SlamJam for supporting a whole lot of this project.
James Lavelle, Toby, Fraser, all people at Mo'Wax for the cuts.
Claudia Tosi and Simona Diacci, capturing the whole action on tape
and Paolo Freschi, editing the monster info suitable form.
Enrico Moretti, for keeping it QTVReal.
Enzo and Paolo Ragazzini for all the printed photographies.
Arch. Chiara Ronchetti, helping with that 3D, and Biccio for the hospitality.
Lara and Max, Osteria Francescana in Modena, the place to be.
Ciao Stash! (Next time ok ?)
Everybody else in Sartoria for keeping up with us during this project.

RELATED:

WWW.INCOSTRUCT.COM
WWW.FUTURA2000.COM

WWW.000MORE.NET   WWW.SLAMJAM.IT
WWW.MOWAX.COM   WWW.SARTORIA.COM

www.defumo.org is a project made in _____ Sartoria = G and Patty kept the project together / Design: Deemo and Fox / Scripting: Bubba Taddeoshi.

SOUNDTRACK courtesy of   SUPPORTED by   MADE in

DESIGNING MUSIC

testi: Damir Ivic

immagini: 3D+Futura 2000
(HEADZ 2 © Mo'Wax, AeM records ltd, London)

Disegnare una rete, e designarla a rappresentarti...
Forse questo gioco di parole può essere un piccolo
scrigno dove trovare i tratti più rappresentativi
della migliore espressività contemporanea... perché
no? Seguendo questa traccia capita di incontrare
nuove isole, provare a legarle con un filo comune
potrebbe risultare importante e significativo.
Potrebbe anche dare un segno all'identità di quella
vera e propria esperienza globale che è la club
culture. L'importante è rendersi conto che se si
vuole fare un viaggio alla scoperta di questi nuovi
territori è molto importante, e anche molto
gratificante, tenere sempre gli occhi aperti e nutrire
sempre la propria curiosità Non più viaggiatori
passivi in ricerca di villaggi vacanze impacchettati,
di all-inclusive tours con tanto di petulante guida;
o meglio, volendo si può fare così... ma di sicuro
si perderanno le cose più belle e le emozioni più
intense, e le isole verranno fuori sfuocate e
indistinte.

Anche i più distratti, là fuori, hanno capito che
qualcosa di grosso è successo in musica, e non solo
nella musica, grazie all'avvento di dj e musica
campionata. Un salto di qualità concettuale oltre
che sonoro. Elementi completamente nuovi sono
nati rimescolando le carte della fruizione artistica.
La musica non fluisce più in un'unica direzione,
ma incomincia ad assumere un andamento a spirale
(una spirale che respira: si allarga e si restringe,
ad lib, non possiamo inquadrarla in modelli

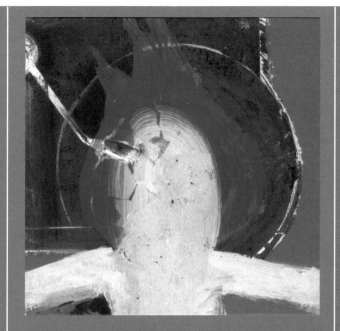

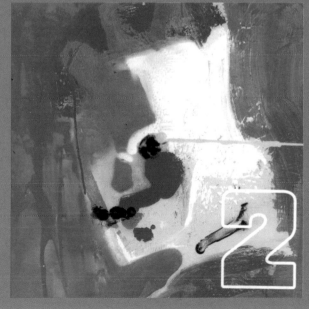

matematici fissi nel tempo e ricorsivi). Sotto forma di
campionatura, musiche passate tornano leggermente
diverse o completamente trasfigurate. Si spezzano i rigidi
confini di spazio e tempo, si spezza la loro attitudine
lineare e unidirezionale (prima isola). Un break di batteria
suonato da Bernard Purdie per James Brown decine di
anni fa, con qualche ritocco può diventare l'impianto
base della musica più futuristica dell'ultimo decennio,
la drum'n'bass, dopo essere stato negli anni '80 la
colonna portante delle produzioni hip hop fondamentali:
basta qualche ritocco di velocità ed equalizzazione per
dargli questo magico potere di durare e rigenerarsi nel
tempo. E questo è solo un esempio fra mille. Se ne volete
un altro, fateci caso: se siete grandi amanti della house
francese è probabile che vi capiti di affermare che in
musica non c'è nulla di più moderno e contemporaneo
degli anni '70... curioso quanto questa frase suoni oggi
tranquillamente ragionevole e logica, no?
Ma andiamo avanti: si spezzano anche le gerarchie
(seconda isola). Una è quella che vuole una netta
distinzione fra creatore e ascoltatore: il pubblico con le
sue reazioni guida spessissimo la scaletta della propria
serata, i dj sono spesso quelli che seducono e al tempo
stesso si fanno sedurre dalle vibrazioni provenienti dal
dancefloor. Un'altra gerarchia che sta cadendo sotto il
peso della sua rigidità è quella fra cultura alta e cultura
bassa, con la musica da ballo che per lungo tempo è stata
confinata esclusivamente entro i confini della seconda -
mero intrattenimento per uno sfogo fisico... ma oggi ciò
quanto può avere senso di fronte alla intensità poetica
dei Massive Attack o all'astrazione di un Dj Krust o alla
grazia cerebrale e cattiva di un Aphex Twin? (Di nuovo,
solo tre esempi di fronte alle migliaia di quelli possibili...).
La spirale di cui parliamo attira su di sé elementi non
solo sonori (terza isola). L'iconicità degli stili è diventata
un elemento imprescindibile, e non potrebbe essere
altrimenti dato il carattere sempre più visuale delle nostre

percezioni quotidiane, dall'invenzione della macchina fotografica in poi. Ciò che ha portato in musica le rivoluzioni del campionamento come regola e del deejaying, ovvero la cultura hip hop, è non a caso portatrice anche della cifra stilistica più forte degli ultimi decenni sia nell'arte (tramite l'aerosol art, comunemente detta graffitismo) che nella moda (sono gli stilisti a vampirizzare ormai i grandi stimoli provenienti dalla strada e non viceversa, per loro stessa ammissione). Etichette che hanno definito nuove vie musicali, come la Talkin' Loud con l'acid jazz e la **Mo' Wax** col trip hop, hanno dato fondamentale importanza alla grafica per darsi un'identità: le raccolte "Headz", pietre miliari del trip hop, non avrebbero lo stesso sapore senza i segni di 3D e Futura 2000, è un dato di fatto.

Una nuova geografia, quindi. Un nuovo modo di esplorarla, circolare e non lineare. Ma le spirali, a non essere pronti ad affrontarle, possono essere pericolose. Danno vertigini. Provare ad imprigionarle nelle care, vecchie, chiare strutture di relazione verticale è impossibile. Proprio per la loro tendenza a muoversi in forme circolari e non inquadrabili definitivamente (la quadratura della circonferenza è ancora uno dei misteri della nostra geometria euclidea, esiste sempre un pi greco di troppo) non avrebbe senso affrontarle in maniera rigida. Esse tendono ad intersecarsi su piani diversi e sempre mutevoli, e di queste ricorsività sempre differenti si nutrono. Meglio quindi non cercare troppe certezze semplici ma imparare a muoversi in rete, dove cioè trasversalismi ed elasticità sono non estemporanee eccezioni ma necessità vitali. Ricordandosi una cosa fondamentale: le reti, proprio per la loro elasticità, offrono un'opportunità unica di costruirsi un proprio itinerario e delle proprie regole, cosa molto più difficile di quanto sembri a prima vista ma molto gratificante. Farlo non è solo uno sfizio, attenzione: creare una rigorosa identità dalla moltitudine di stimoli che ci seduce è la nostra arma contro il collasso da troppa contingenza e troppa quantità. Siamo umani, abbiamo le nostre passioni, le nostre preclusioni e i nostri limiti: dobbiamo ricordarci di non cadere nella trappola del desiderio di accumulazione indistinta ed infinita, queste utopie ad una dimensione meglio lasciarle nei giochi speculativi delle borse di tutto il mondo, quella è la loro dimensione (e pure lì, vanno tenute sotto controllo). Il viaggio a isole e l'affascinante imprevedibilità delle spirali deve servire non a nutrire una bulimia emozionale bensì a darci strumenti per sorridere e stare nel mondo che noi (sì, proprio noi) ci stiamo costruendo giorno dopo giorno, passo dopo passo, partendo dalle piccole cose che con maggior naturalezza sentiamo vicine (a partire, perché no?, dalle calde serate passate fra le vibrazioni positive di un club…).

Disegnare una rete, e designarla a rappresentarti…

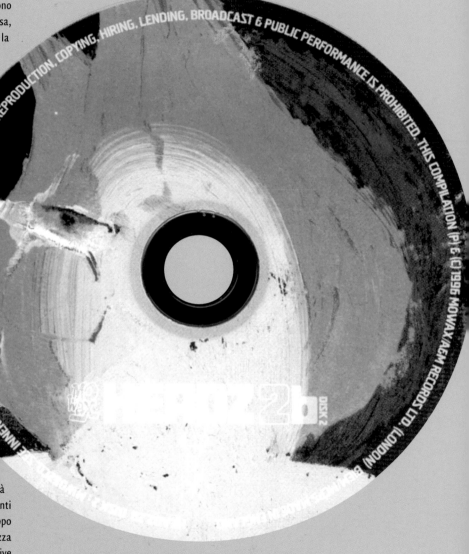

INNER SLEEVE FOR DETAILS. ALL RIGHTS RESERVED. UNAUTHORISED REPRODUCTION, COPYING, HIRING, LENDING, BROADCAST & PUBLIC PERFORMANCE IS PROHIBITED. THIS COMPILATION (P) & (C)1996 MO'WAX/A&M RECORDS LTD. (LONDON)

3D+Futura 2000
(HEADZ 2 © Mo'Wax, A&M records ltd. Lon

SUB @ FLEX
wien, austria

www.sub.sil.at

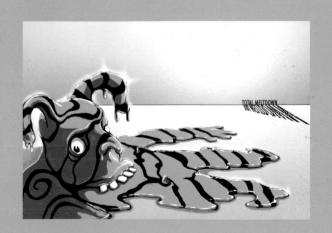

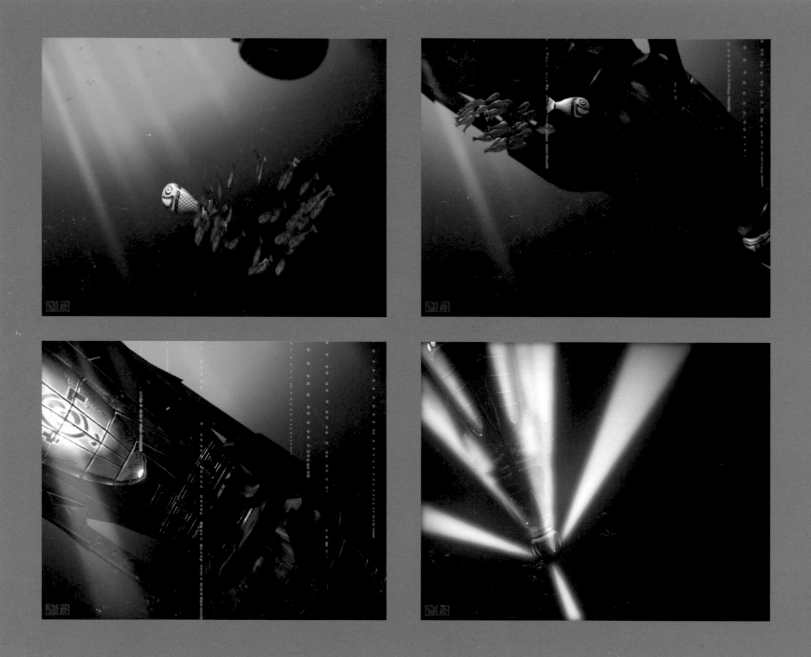

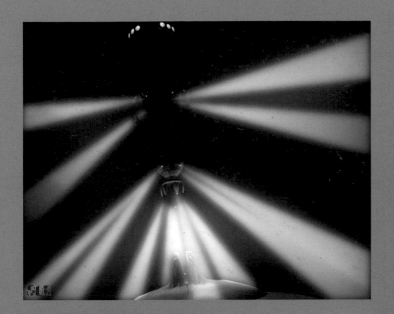

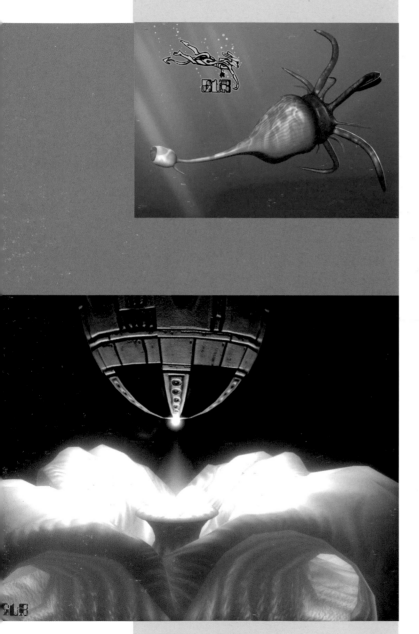

LUXFRÁGIL
lisbon, portugal

www.luxfragil.com

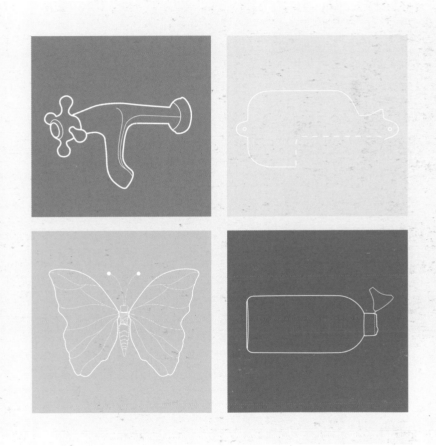

designer:
Jorge Ramalho
Jonathan Beach
Ricardo Mealha
Ana Cunha

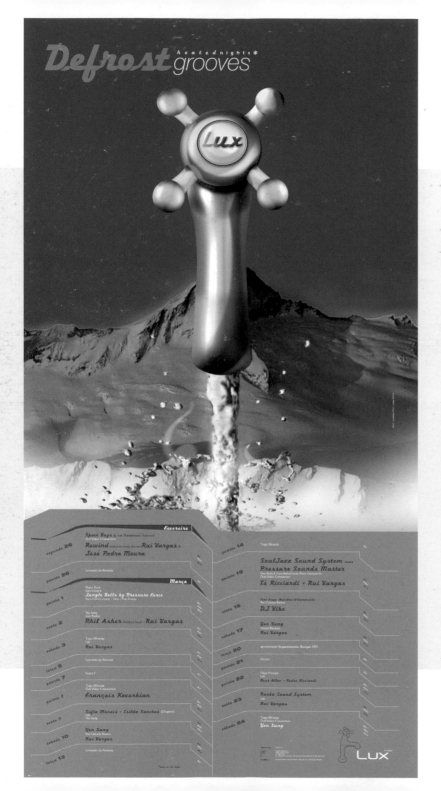

OM
cais dos soldados (lisboa)
TAXA PAGA

AUTORIZADO A CIRCULAR FECHADO
Pode abrir-se para verificação postal

3

-/ Av. Infante D. Henrique, Armazém A, Cais da Pedra a Sta. Apolónia

LUX

Night Tanning
DANCEFLOOR MOISTURISER

(Abril

24 Terça	bar video disco	Tiago Miranda Rui Calçada Bastos **Rui Vargas**
26 Quinta	bar video disco	Dexter Lab Image Dpt. **Jungle Bells by Pressure Force** Nuno Forte (Looping) + Dinis Filipa Príncipe + mc Bezego
27 Sexta	bar video disco	Tozé Diogo (Bassline/Urbansound) Dub Video Connection **DJ Vibe**
28 Sábado	bar video disco	Yen Sung João Vinagre **Rui Vargas**
30 Segunda	bar video disco	Tiago Miranda + Filipa Príncipe José Budha **Yen Sung**

N° [0000]

N° [0000]

2500$ (IVA incluido)

06

sexta ao vivo **22.30 h**

ESG

plus **megafone** *(1ªparte)*

spring *departures*

fly with me

LUX
frágil

Setembro no Lux

o9.oo

31.o8   José Pedro Moura + Dinis   Quinta

o2.o9   Rui Vargas   Sábado

Set/Outubro no Lux

1o.oo

o3.1o   **St Germain** ao vivo   Terça

ZOUK

83
96

Flyer*zone

singapore

www.zoukclub.com

ZOUK and GOETHE INSTITUT present a week of

BERLIN MUSIC *AND* CLUB CULTURE

JAZZANOVA (DJ set)

Date	Wednesday 6 December 2000
Time	10.30pm
Venue	**Velvet Underground** 17 Jiak Kim Street S169420
Price	normal admission charges

DJ BLEED aka SASCHA KOSCH (drum n bass)

Date	Saturday 9 December 2000
Time	12 midnight
Venue	**Phuture** 17 Jiak Kim Street S169420
Price	normal admission charges

SEMINAR ON MUSIC AND CLUB CULTURE IN BERLIN AND SINGAPORE

Date	Saturday 9 December 2000
Time	3.00pm
Venue	**Goethe-Institut** 163 Penang Road #05-01 Winsland House II S238463
Price	free admission if you wish to attend, please register with Tracy Phillips of Zouk Managemnt
Hosted by	Jurgen von Knoblauch. Alexander Barck, and Claas Brieler (Jazzanova) Sascha Kosch and Mercedes Bunz (De:Bug Magazine)

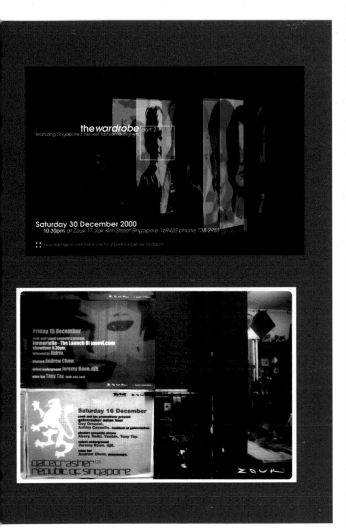

the *wardrobe* part 2
featuring Singapore's newest fashion designers

Saturday 30 December 2000
10.30pm at Zouk 17 Jiak Kim Street Singapore 169420 phone 738 2988

Free admission with this invite for 2 persons before 10.00pm

Friday 15 December
zouk and i spaci cosmetics present
immortelle - The Launch Of insevt.com
showtime 9.30pm.
followed by **Aldrin.**
phuture **Andrew Chow.**
velvet underground **Jeremy Boon. djB.**
wine bar **Tony Tay.** funk and soul

Saturday 16 December
zouk and tsc promotions present
gatecrasher asian tour
Guy Ornadel.
Ashley Casselle. resident at gatecrasher.
phuture residents' nite
Abery. Relkl. Yonbin. Tony Tay.
velvet underground
Jeremy Boon. djB.
wine bar
Andrew Chow. downtempo.

gatecrasher b.m.
republic of singapore

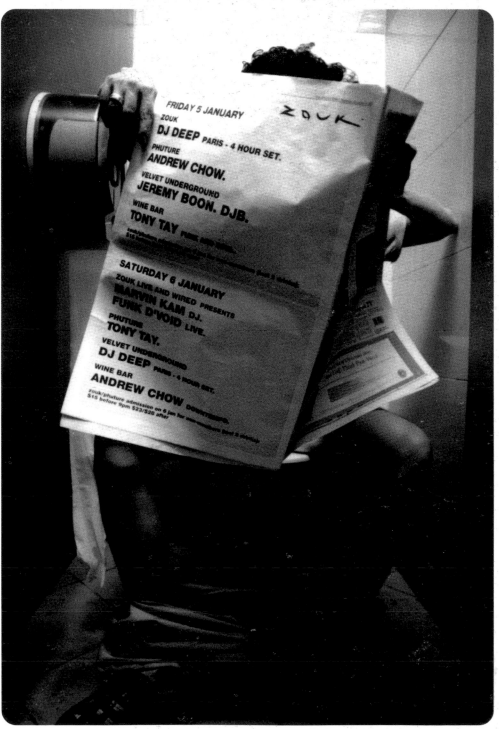

FRIDAY 5 JANUARY
ZOUK
DJ DEEP PARIS - 4 HOUR SET.
PHUTURE
ANDREW CHOW.
VELVET UNDERGROUND
JEREMY BOON. DJB.
WINE BAR
TONY TAY. FUNK AND SOUL.

SATURDAY 6 JANUARY
ZOUK LIVE AND WIRED PRESENTS
MARVIN KAM DJ.
FUNK D'VOID LIVE.
PHUTURE
TONY TAY.
VELVET UNDERGROUND
DJ DEEP PARIS - 4 HOUR SET.
WINE BAR
ANDREW CHOW DOWNTEMPO.

zouk/phuture admission on 6 jan
$15 before 9pm $23/$26 after

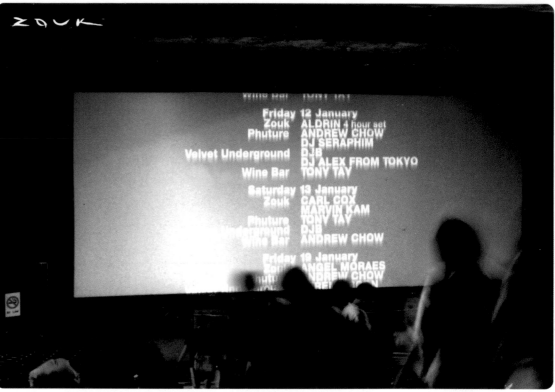

Friday 12 January
Zouk ALDRIN 4 hour set
Phuture ANDREW CHOW
DJ SERAPHIM
Velvet Underground DJB
DJ ALEX FROM TOKYO
Wine Bar TONY TAY

Saturday 13 January
Zouk CARL COX
MARVIN KAM
Phuture TONY TAY
Underground DJB
Wine Bar ANDREW CHOW

Friday 19 January
Zouk ANGEL MORAES
Phuture ANDREW CHOW

WELCOME TO GREAT W

ZOUK

29 DECEMBER
30 DECEMBER

FRIDAY
zouk Roger Sanchez 4 hour set.
phuture Andrew Chow.
velvet Jeremy Boon.
wine bar Tony Tay funk and soul.

SATURDAY
zouk presents the wardrobe part 2
Comprehensive metaphorical structure free /
mizu Spring 2001 showtime 10.30pm.
followed by Marvin Kam.
phuture Tony Tay, Freq Nasty.
velvet Jeremy Boon. djB.
wine bar Andrew Chow downtempo.

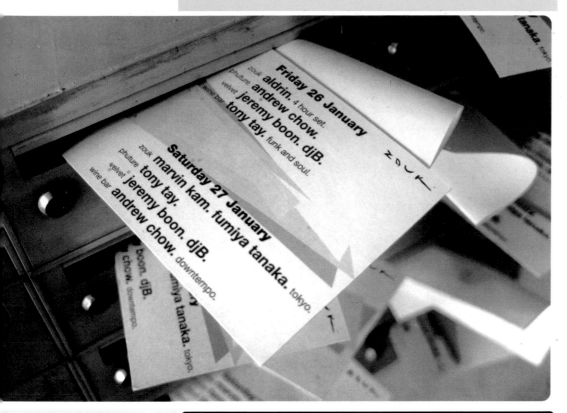

Friday 26 January
zouk **aldrin.** 4 hour set.
phuture **andrew chow.**
velvet **jeremy boon. djB.**
wine bar **tony tay.** funk and soul.

Saturday 27 January
zouk **marvin kam. fumiya tanaka.** tokyo.
phuture **tony tay.**
velvet **jeremy boon. djB.**
wine bar **andrew chow.** downtempo.

Friday 8 December
zouk live and wired presents
Aldrin dj.
Swayzak live.

phuture
Andrew Chow.

velvet underground
Jeremy Boon. djB.

wine bar
Tony Tay funk and soul.

Saturday 9 December
zouk
Trigger 2nd Birthday starting at 9.00pm
followed by **Marvin Kam.**

phuture and the goethe-institut singapur
present berlin music and club culture
Tony Tay. DJ Bleed aka Sascha Kosch drum n bass.

velvet underground
Norman Jay. Bruno café del mar - ibiza.

wine bar
Andrew Chow downtempo.

first dj at zouk of
The Real Millennium

happy new year

GLOBALUNDERGROUND presents

DARREN**EMERSON**

Darren Emerson needs little introduction. Although best known for once being a member of Underworld, he is a renowned DJ and label owner in his own right. He heads up a small underground label of his own - Underwater Records - and earlier this year took clubbers by storm with "Scorchio", his tasty collaboration with Sasha. His DJing skills are always much in demand, these days this is especially true in America. His ability to mingle coolly rumbling house music with funky, jazzy techno, as shown in his latest Global Underground CD, makes him defy what people have pigeon-holed him to be. Darren is the ideal DJ to bring in the new millennium at Zouk.

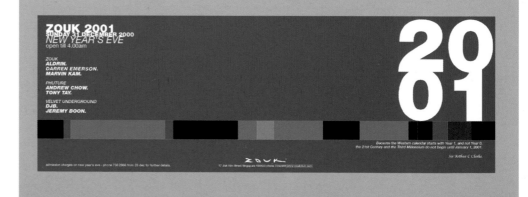

ZOUK 2001
SUNDAY 31 DECEMBER 2000
NEW YEAR'S EVE
open till 4.00am

ZOUK
**ALDRIN.
DARREN EMERSON.
MARVIN KAM.**

PHUTURE
**ANDREW CHOW.
TONY TAY.**

VELVET UNDERGROUND
**DJB.
JEREMY BOON.**

2001

Because the Western calendar starts with Year 1, and not Year 0,
the 21st Century and the Third Millennium do not begin until January 1, 2001.

Sir Arthur C Clarke

admission charges on new year's eve - phone 738 2988 from 25 dec for further details.

ZOUK
17 Jiak Kim Street Singapore 169420 phone 7382988 www.zoukclub.com

FIREWORKS and **ZOUK** invite you to

THE FLYING CIRCUS PROJECT:00 CLOSING PARTY

japanese club culture featuring
toru yamanaka ::: yen ::: yoshiide otomo
thursday 21 december at zouk
starting at 9.00pm

FREE ADMISSION WITH THIS INVITE
FOR 2 PERSONS BEFORE 9.30PM

toro yamanaka [to-ro-ya-ma-na-ka] *n.* a computer musician who is the main collaborator of teiji / dumb type productions.

yen [y-en] *n.* a pop vocalist who has experimented with unconventional ways of voice production. combined commercial music production and avant garde singing heavily inspired by middle eastern / moorish music.

yoshiide otomo [yo-shi-i-de-o-to-mo] *n.* a turntablist / dj who experiments with the turntable as a sound instrument. of late, much of his work has concentrated in experimental concerts in europe where he collaborates with other sound artists from the continent.

LAW AND THE MEDIA

Tuesday and **Friday nights** at the Zouk Wine Bar
all drinks 1 for 1 all night in the Wine Bar for those in the law and media/advertising industries
plus on Tuesday nights only, free entry to Velvet Underground with your business card

The Zouk Wine Bar opens nightly from 6.00pm to 9.00pm

ZOUK 17 jiak kim street singapore 169420 phone 7382380 www.zoukclub.com.sg

breaks and beats
sat 16.09.00
at phuture

Abery · 11.00pm
Reiki · 12.00am
Yanbin · 01.00am
Tony Tay · 02.00am

free entry with this flyer before 10.30pm

ZOUK

ZOUK

friday08092000
zouk
Jonathan Yeo. Dimitri From Paris.

phuture
Andrew Chow.

velvet underground
Jeremy Boon.

wine bar
Tony Tay funk and soul.

zouk/phuture 8 sep admission for non-members (incl 2 drinks) :
$18 before 9pm $25/$30 after

saturday09092000
zouk
Jonathan Yeo.

phuture
Tony Tay.

velvet underground
Marvin Kam.

wine bar
Andrew Chow downtempo.

zouk/phuture saturday admission for non-members (incl 2 drinks) :
$12 before 9pm $20/$25 after

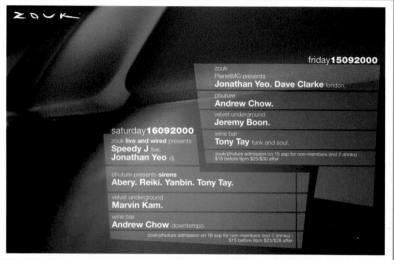

ZOUK

friday15092000
zouk
PlanetMG presents
Jonathan Yeo. Dave Clarke london.

phuture
Andrew Chow.

velvet underground
Jeremy Boon.

wine bar
Tony Tay funk and soul.

zouk/phuture admission on 15 sep for non-members (incl 2 drinks) :
$18 before 9pm $25/$30 after

saturday16092000
zouk **live and wired** presents
Speedy J live
Jonathan Yeo dj.

phuture presents **sirens**
Abery. Reiki. Yanbin. Tony Tay.

velvet underground
Marvin Kam.

wine bar
Andrew Chow downtempo.

zouk/phuture admission on 16 sep for non-members (incl 2 drinks) :
$15 before 9pm $23/$28 after

ZOUK

friday22092000
zouk
Aldrin.

phuture
Andrew Chow.

velvet underground
Jeremy Boon.

wine bar
Tony Tay funk and soul.

zouk/phuture friday admission for non-members (incl 2 drinks) :
$12 before 9pm $20/$25 after

saturday23092000
zouk and club [V] present
John Digweed 4 hour set

club[V]

phuture
Tony Tay.

velvet underground
Marvin kam.

wine bar
Andrew Chow downtempo.

zouk/phuture admission on 23 sep for non-members (incl 2 drinks) :
$28/$33 on sale from 8 sep at the zouk ticketing booth (open tue-sat 7pm-3am)
zouk complimentary members cannot sign in guests on this night.

invites you to

the wardrobe
featuring singapore's newest fashion designers

part 1 - the encapsulated apocalyptic picnic
capsule by alfie leong   tyclub by terence yeong   d.po by teresa koh

saturday 25 november 2000
10.30pm at zouk

free admission with this invite for 2 persons before 10.00pm

Friday**03112000**
and zouk present the san francisco sessions pt 1.
Dano. JZ redmelon records - 4 hour set.
phuture
Andrew Chow.
velvet underground
Jeremy Boon.

Saturday**04112000**
zouk
Marvin Kam.
phuture
Andrew Chow.
velvet underground
Jeremy Boon.

Friday**06102000**
zouk
Smirnoff Fashion Awards. 2000 Singapore Final.
showtime 9.30pm.
Aldrin. Joe Claussell Resident at Body & Soul, New York.
phuture
Andrew Chow.
velvet underground
Jeremy Boon.

Saturday**07102000**
zouk and planetMG present
Jonathan Yeo. Jeff Mills Detroit.
phuture
Andrew Chow.
velvet underground
Marvin Kam.

Friday**20102000**
zouk
Aldrin.

phuture
Andrew Chow.

velvet underground
Jeremy Boon.

zouk/phuture friday admission for non-members (incl 2 drinks).
$12 before 9pm $20/$28 after

Saturday**21102000**
zouk and maniac love present
Jonathan Yeo. DJ Shufflemaster Tokyo.

phuture
Andrew Chow.

velvet underground
Marvin Kam.

zouk/phuture admission on 21 oct for non-members (incl 2 drinks)
$15 before 9pm $23/$28 after

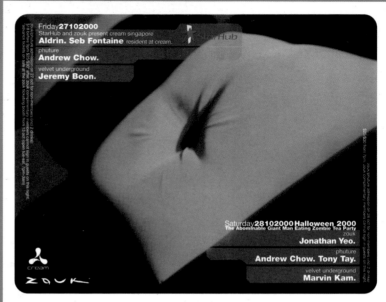

Friday**27102000**
StarHub and zouk present cream·singapore
Aldrin. Seb Fontaine resident at cream.

phuture
Andrew Chow.

velvet underground
Jeremy Boon.

Saturday**28102000 Halloween 2000**
The Abominable Giant Man Eating Zombie Tea Party
zouk
Jonathan Yeo.

phuture
Andrew Chow. Tony Tay.

velvet underground
Marvin Kam.

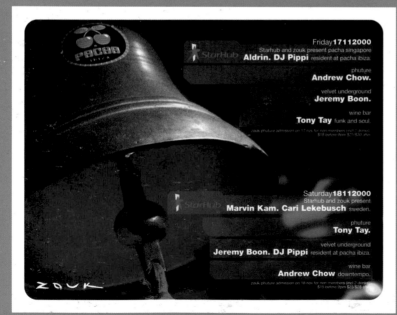

Friday**17112000**
Starhub and zouk present pacha singapore
Aldrin. DJ Pippi resident at pacha ibiza.

phuture
Andrew Chow.

velvet underground
Jeremy Boon.

wine bar
Tony Tay funk and soul.

zouk phuture admission on 17 nov for non-members (incl 2 drinks)
$18 before door $25/$30 after

Saturday**18112000**
Starhub and zouk present.
Marvin Kam. Cari Lekebusch sweden.

phuture
Tony Tay.

velvet underground
Jeremy Boon. DJ Pippi resident at pacha ibiza.

wine bar
Andrew Chow downtempo.

zouk phuture admission on 18 nov for non members (incl 2 drinks)
$15 before 9pm $23/$28 after

Friday**10112000**
zouk
**Tery Lee & Double Helix present The Joint -
the follow up to Room 117**
showtime 9.30pm - followed by **Aldrin.**

phuture
Andrew Chow.

velvet underground
Jeremy Boon.

wine bar
Tony Tay funk and soul.

Saturday**11112000**
zouk
Marvin Kam.

phuture
Tony Tay.

velvet underground
Jeremy Boon.

wine bar
Andrew Chow downtempo.

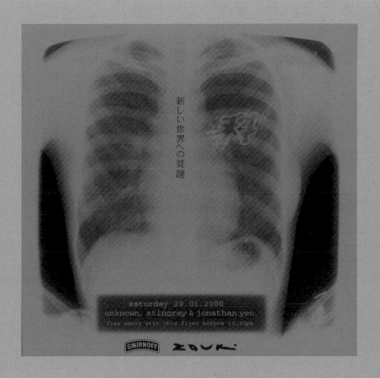

新しい世界への覚醒

saturday 29.01.2000
unknown, stingray & jonathan yeo
free entry with this flyer before 10.30pm

SMIRNOFF ZOUK

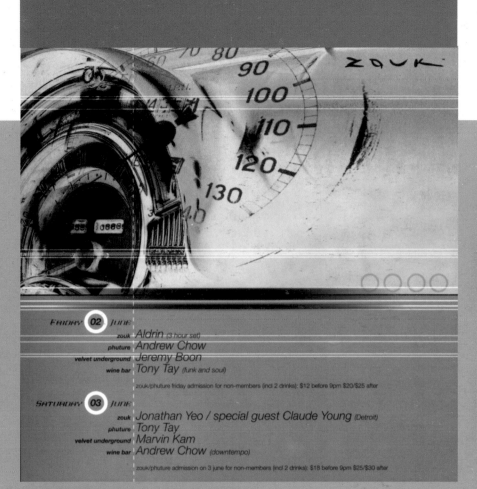

ZOUK

FRIDAY 02 JUNE

zouk	Aldrin *(3 hour set)*
phuture	Andrew Chow
velvet underground	Jeremy Boon
wine bar	Tony Tay *(funk and soul)*

zouk/phuture friday admission for non-members (incl 2 drinks): $12 before 9pm $20/$25 after

SATURDAY 03 JUNE

zouk	Jonathan Yeo / special guest Claude Young *(Detroit)*
phuture	Tony Tay
velvet underground	Marvin Kam
wine bar	Andrew Chow *(downtempo)*

zouk/phuture admission on 3 june for non-members (incl 2 drinks): $18 before 9pm $25/$30 after

FRI 09.06.00   SAT 10.06.00

GLOBALUNDERGROUND nubreed TOUR

zouk	Aldrin/special guest Anthony Pappa *(melbourne/london)*	zouk	Jonathan Yeo *(4 hour set)*
phuture	Andrew Chow	phuture	Tony Tay
velvet underground	Jeremy Boon	velvet underground	Marvin Kam
wine bar	Tony Tay *(funk and soul)*	wine bar	Andrew Chow *(downtempo)*

zouk/phuture admission on 9 jun for non-members (incl 2 drinks): $18 before 9pm $25/$30 after

zouk/phuture Saturday admission for non-members (incl 2 drinks): $12 before 9pm $20/$25 after

ZOUK

ZOUK

zouk special guest sasha (4 hour set)
phuture andrew chow
velvet underground tangs summer collection featuring a special appearance by
ralph lauren polo sport model tyson beckford
showtime 10.30pm - followed by jeremy boon
wine bar tony tay (funk and soul) zouk/phuture admission on 21 jul for non-members (incl 2 drinks): $28/$33
on sale from 12 jul at the zouk ticketing booth (open tue-sat, 7pm-3am)

FRI21JULY **SAT**22JULY

zouk jonathan yeo
phuture tony tay
velvet underground marvin kam
wine bar andrew chow (downtempo)
zouk/phuture saturday admission for non-members (incl 2 drinks):
$12 before 9pm $20/$25 after

03/08

zouk

FRI30JUNE zouk/phuture friday admission for non-members (incl 2 drinks):
$12 before 9pm $20/$25 after
zouk **Woods & Woods** Autumn/Winter '00-'01
showtime 10.00pm - followed by aldrin
phuture andrew chow
velvet underground marvin kam
wine bar tony tay (funk and soul)

01/08

kē: new world conscience

turday05082000

chnasia
an deans
cuffy
oject eastward
uis
at
ndie
mesh
ny tay
nathan yeo

www.kefm.net

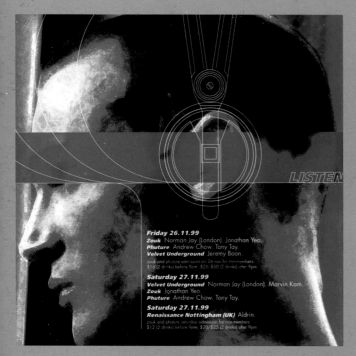

Friday 26.11.99

Zouk Norman Jay (London). Jonathan Yeo.
Phuture Andrew Chow. Tony Tay.
Velvet Underground Jeremy Boon.

zouk and phuture admission on 26 nov for non-members:
$18 (2 drinks) before 9pm $25. $30 (2 drinks) after 9pm

Saturday 27.11.99

Velvet Underground Norman Jay (London). Marvin Kam.
Zouk Jonathan Yeo.
Phuture Andrew Chow. Tony Tay.

Saturday 27.11.99

Renaissance Nottingham (UK) Aldrin.

zouk and phuture saturday admission for non-members:
$12 (2 drinks) before 9pm $20/$25 (2 drinks) after 9pm

ZOUK

friday29092000
zouk presents tyrant
Lee Burridge. Craig Richards 4 hour set.
phuture
Andrew Chow.
velvet underground
Jeremy Boon.
wine bar
Tony Tay funk and soul.

saturday30092000
zouk
Surgeon. James Ruskin 4 hour set.
phuture
Tony Tay.
velvet underground
Marvin Kam.
wine bar
Andrew Chow downtempo.

zouk/phuture admission on 29 sep for non-members (incl 2 drinks): $18 before 9pm $25/$30* after.
zouk complimentary members cannot sign in guests on this night.

*advance tickets on sale at the zouk ticketing booth from 20 sep (open tue-sat, 7pm-3am)

zouk/phuture admission on 30 sep for non-members (incl 2 drinks):
$15 before 9pm $23/$28 after.

Friday 03.12.99

Zouk Triggerfish - 1st Birthday Party
starting at 9.00pm - followed by Jonathan Yeo.
Phuture Andrew Chow. Tony Tay.
Velvet Underground Jeremy Boon.

Saturday 04.12.99

Zouk Concave Scream - "Three" Album Launch Party
starting at 9.00pm - followed by Jonathan Yeo.
Phuture Sessions, starting at 10.00pm.
Velvet Underground Marvin Kam.

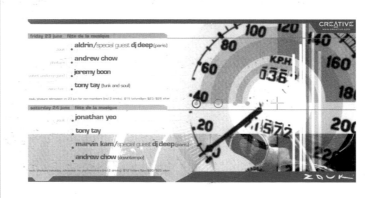

CREATIVE

friday 23 june fête de la musique

zouk   **aldrin**/special guest: **dj deep** (paris)
phuture   **andrew chow**
velvet underground   **jeremy boon**
              tony tay (funk and soul)

zouk/phuture admission on 23 jun for non-members (incl 2 drinks). $15 before 9pm $23/$28 after

saturday 24 june fête de la musique

zouk   **jonathan yeo**
              tony tay
              marvin kam/special guest: **dj deep** (paris)
              andrew chow (downtempo)

ZOUK

DINAMO-DVASH
tel aviv, israel

www.dinamo-dvash.co.il

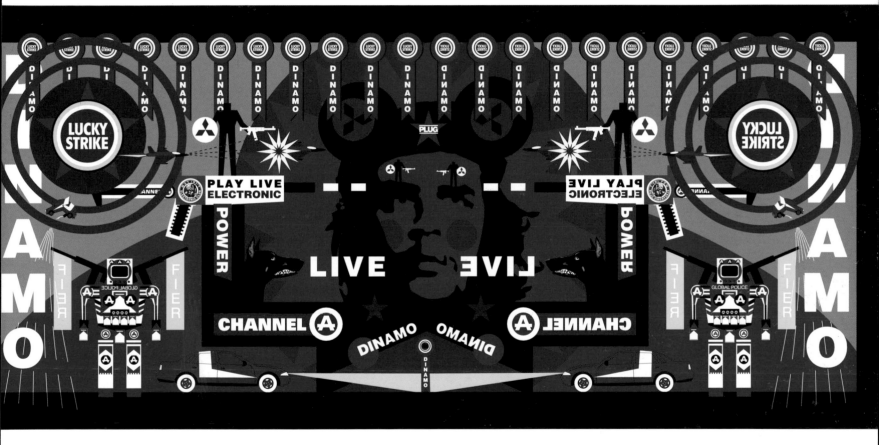

dinamo art squad:
Ido Shemi (art director)
Vadim Levin
Eyal B
Flashkes
Channel A design
Mushon Zer-Aviv (web designer)

DINAMO DVASH
SUPER ELECTRONIC CLUB
I S R A E L

WWW.DINAMO-DVASH.CO.IL

ABARBANEL 59 TEL-AVIV ISRAEL 66
TEL: 972-3-6829937 TELFAX:972-3-683515

DJ O-Fear
DJ Nir Segal

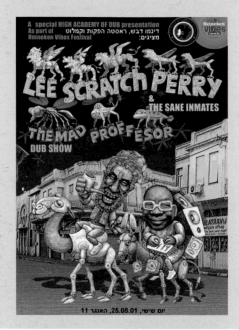

A special HIGH ACADEMY OF DUB presentation
As part of Heineken Vibes Festival

דינמו דבש, ראסטה הפקות וקמליט
מציגים:

LEE SCRATCH PERRY
& THE SANE INMATES

THE MAD PROFFESOR

DUB SHOW

יום שישי, 25.05.01, האנגר 11

DINAMO DVASH
ABRBANEL 59
STANGA
WWW.DINAMO-DVASH.CO.IL

MICHAEL DOG
(PLANET DOG -U.K)
D.J E
round#2
FRIDAY freestyle
21.5.99 24:00

ELECTRIC BEAPS TO ACID TECHNO
DJ MELOMANIAC
Friday 24:00
18.2.2000

DYNAMIC DJ'S COMMANDO
DOBBERMAN
ANTWERP BELGIE
DJ MASHA
Friday 24:00
21.1.2000

DINAMO DVASH
Abarbanel 59
drum'n'bass
d.j. E
d.j Wow d.j Yem
d.j. Adi Lev
Thursday
27.5.99 24:00

DINAMO DVASH
Abarbanel 59
"SATURDAY NIGHT LIVE"
Shantel
(Frankfurt)
EASSY RECORDINGS
Saturday
1.5.99 24:00

DINAMO DVASH
Abarbanel 59
A Kick in the eye...or shake them hips
Thursday
13.5.99 24:30
Shantel & Haaksman
(Frankfurt -Berlin)
EASSY RECORDINGS

DINAMO DVASH
Abarbanel 59
round #1 Jungle
Michael Dog
Planet Dog-London
d.j. E
Thursday
20.5.99 24:00

ראסטה הפקות ודינמו דבש גאים להציג: סדרת הדאב החודשית של ה
STANGA
יום שישי
THE HIGH ACADEMY OF DUB
24:00, 16.02.2001.

GABRE SELASSIE

UP, BUSTLE & OUT
(Ninja Tune, UK)

דינמו דבש

מציג אוקטובר 2000

אברבנל 59 תל - אביב

tel:03-6829937 telefax:03-6835159
dinamo_dvash@hotmail.com

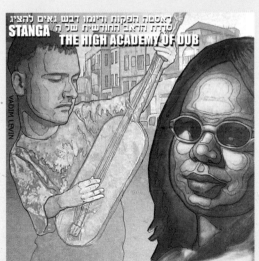

לאסטה הפקות ודינמו דבש גאים להציג
סדרת הדאב החודשית של ה
STANGA
THE HIGH ACADEMY OF DUB

VADIM LEVIN

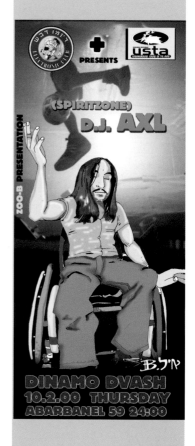

D.J. O-FEAR
D.J. SHELIAK
(BASSLINE RECORDS) FRANCE
GUEST-D.J. YAYA

PRESENTS

D.J.PHILIP
(VooV expirience) GERMANY
+
USTA D.J.S'

DINAMO DVASH
30.3.00 THURSDAY
ABARBANEL 59 24:00

DINAMO DVASH PRESENTS THE OUTRAGEOUS PURIM PARTY

OUTBREAK VS DANSHA
+ D.J. הרא

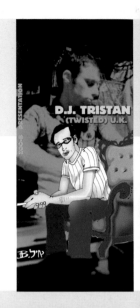

D.J. TRISTAN
(TWISTED) U.K.

ZOO-S PRESENTATION

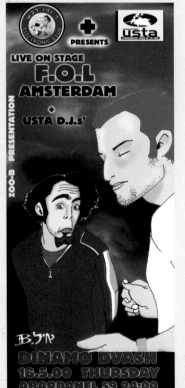

ELECTRONIC CLUB + usta PRESENTS

LIVE ON STAGE
F.O.L
AMSTERDAM
+
USTA D.J.s'

ZOO-B PRESENTATION

DINAMO DVASH
18.5.00 THURSDAY
ABARBANEL 59 24:00

ABARBANEL 59 TEL AVIV   03 6835159
DINAMO DVASH PROUDLY PRESENTS

THURSDAY 25.11.99
D.J. YANIV (COSMOPHILIA-GERMANY)
YAKOV BITON (spiral activ)
D.J. O-FEAR

FRIDAY 26.11.99
D.J MELOMANIAC
(TRANCENTRAL,LONDON)
D.J. AVNER

FRIDAY 3.12.99
D.J. KAOS
(TERRANOVA K-7) BERLIN
D.J. NADAV RAVID

E-Flyers
www.dinamo-dvash.co.il

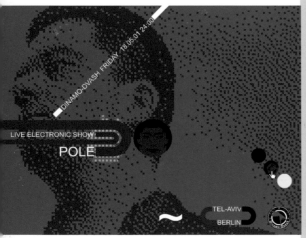

LIVE ELECTRONIC SHOW
POLE

DINAMO-DVASH FRIDAY 18.06.01 24:00

TEL-AVIV
BERLIN

DJ SET
BARBARA PREISINGER

TEL-AV
BERLIN

LIVE ELECTRONIC SHOW
JAN JELINEK

TEL-AVIV
BERLIN

friday.27>4>01

The British Council

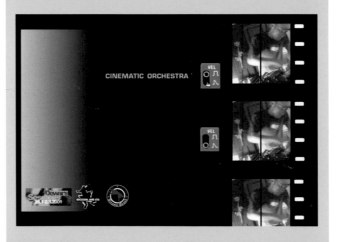

CINEMATIC ORCHESTRA

@ the

go to tal's
website

Tal (Subrosa)

הלייבל הבלתי **Subrosa**, ללא ספק אחד הנופים המוטיקלייט
המעניינים והמאתגרים ביותר באירופה כיום, עם אומנים כמו
Bill Laswel, **David Shea** ו **DJ Spooky** מבין רבים,
Subrosa הוא קרקע פורייה ליצירה אלקטרונית מתקדמת.

במסגרת שיתוף פעולה הולך ומתפתח בין הדינמו דבש

English

SATO LABO
Satoshi Matsuzawa
japan

Please introduce yourself
My name is Satoshi Matsuzawa. I live near Tokyo. I work as an illustrator besides being a web designer. Mainly, I do illustrations for CD covers, magazines, posters and Web sites.

What is SatoLabo?
There isn't much meaning in the name of SatoLabo. It's Sato(shi)'s Labo(ratory). In the beginning, I did this site only for myself; without a job; just like my selfish "Laboratory". Now, I get some jobs from this site.

What do you like about what you're doing?
I'm inspired by "Lupin the Third," a Japanese 70's animation. Besides that, I don't really like animation. But I do like 60's and 70's movies. Plus, I don't adhere to be an illustrator or animator.

What do you like about 60's and 70's design?
I love it! The greatest works are Blue Note album covers by Reid Miles. And I love the Archigram artists of the 60's. The 60's and the 70's had the consciousness of "future" in the designs, whether they were in movies, music, products or cultures. To me, that's powerful.

What do you like about Japan? What do you hate about Japan?
That's difficult for me to answer. I like Japan because I was born here. I hate Japan for its business style. There's too much work! And I hate any Japanese product designs... too many switches!

What would you do if you were not an illustrator?
Maybe, an engineer. I studied mechanical engineering at a university. However, I don't remember what I've learned.

Favorites?
007 series for favorite movies. "Goldfinger" is the best one. "Mission: Impossible" for favorite TV show. I also like Jean-Luc Godard's films and any other Nouvelberg films. Of course, films of Wim Venders -- "Paris, Texas" is the best. I like too many kinds of music. From jazz to soul to even movie soundtracks.

What's the reaction like to SatoLabo?
Since opening SatoLabo, I've gotten messages from all over the world. I'm very happy that there are a lot of people who like my stuff. I also got the funniest e-mail two years ago from some Chilean enterprise. They misunderstood and thought that I was a real spy! Maybe they only read the title "Spy-Book" which is my message board. They also mistook my Japanese words for some sort of code. I received a blame mail about that.

"satoshi interview by: cia_b for generationrice.com"

"557"
Copyright 2001
Satoshi Matsuzawa
All Rights Reserved.

"DIGIMU 5"
Copyright 2001
Satoshi Matsuzawa
All Rights Reserved.

SUPERNOVA

"Supernova"
Copyright 2001
Satoshi Matsuzawa
All Rights Reserved.

illustration

Satoshi
Matsuzawa

"Orange Marmalade"
Copyright 2001
Satoshi Matsuzawa
All Rights Reserved.

"Spy Girl"
Copyright 2001
Satoshi Matsuzawa
All Rights Reserved.

"Target"
Copyright 2001
Satoshi Matsuzawa
All Rights Reserved.

"Cool Chasers"
Copyright 2001
Satoshi Matsuzawa
All Rights Reserved.

"Wallpapers"
Copyright 2001
Satoshi Matsuzawa
All Rights Reserved.

"THE SLOT"

"The Slot"
Copyright 2001
Satoshi Matsuzawa
All Rights Reserved.

e STATION

SHIBUYA

"E-Station"
Copyright 2001
Satoshi Matsuzawa
All Rights Reserved.

Azure Lounge

featuring Little Big bee

Mint Lounge

featuring
SATOSHI HIDAKA
DJ TURBO
(GTS)

Yellow Lounge

featuring
Stylus meets DJ KEY

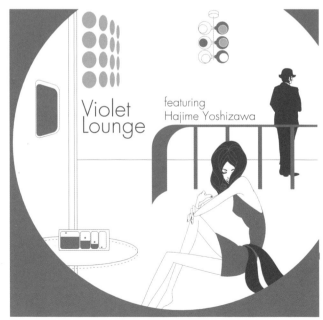

Violet Lounge

featuring
Hajime Yoshizawa

"Cover CD"
Copyright 2001
Satoshi Matsuzawa
All Rights Reserved.

White
Lounge
featuring 01 a.k.a. bayaka

"Zero-one"
Copyright 2001
Satoshi Matsuzawa
All Rights Reserved.

"Virago"
Copyright 2001
Satoshi Matsuzawa
All Rights Reserved.

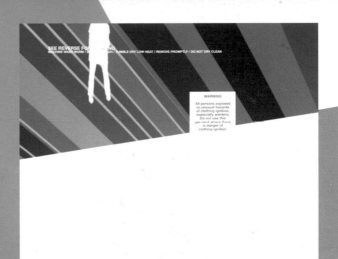

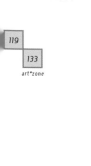

ROBERTO BAGATTI

italy

born in london (11.01.1971)
grew up in london, milan and parma
Interests range from the history of
art to the history of cinema, music,
design and whatever leads to
communication

WORK EXPERIENCE:

1999 - present
MTV EUROPE - ITALY
milan

1991 - 1999
Freelance typographer,
print design
Mc Cann Erickson Milan
Leo Burnett, milan

EXHIBITIONS:

PURPLE 8 1/2
Jousse Seguin Gallery
Paris, 1996

BAGATTI, BOGGIO SELLA, TORENO
Analix Gallery
geneve, 1997

CLUBSPOTTING 2000
A journey into club culture
reggio emilia, italy

PUBLISHED WORKS:

Art in America,
Purple Prose,
Flash Art, Virus

EXTREME FONTS
By S. Drate & J. Salavetz
Gingko press, Hamburg 1999

CLUBSPOTTING
A journey into club culture
By P. Davoli & G. Fantuzzi
Happy books, italy

**Fashionably Loud
Europe**
MTV Europe
20''
2001

STYLE

STYLE

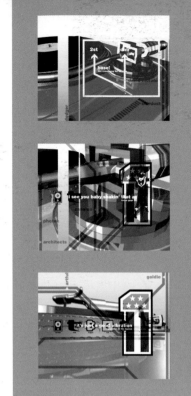

house your **use your body**

strike it up!

alert   pac man   private

demon

frankie knuckles

pump up the volume

strike it up!

alert   pac man   private

luke vibert

pump up the volume
strike it up!

move your body

MTV

Channel Identity
(Dance)
MTV Italy
5'' + 3''
2001

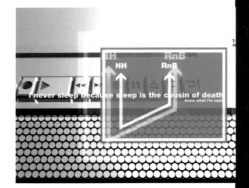

Channel Identity
(Hip-Hop)
MTV Italy
5'' + 3''
2001

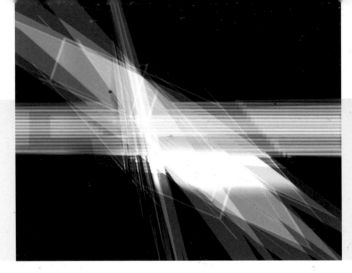

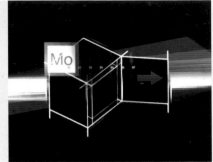

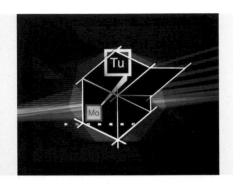

Week In Rock
(designer's cut)
MTV Italy
15''
2000

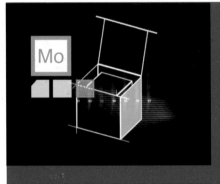

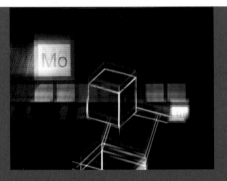

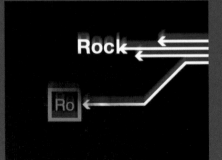

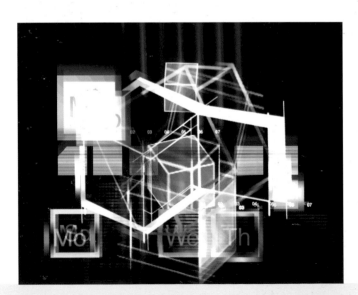

UNA PRODUZIONE RETE EUROPA/MTV PRODUCTION © MTV NETWORKS 2001. ALL RIGHTS RESERVED

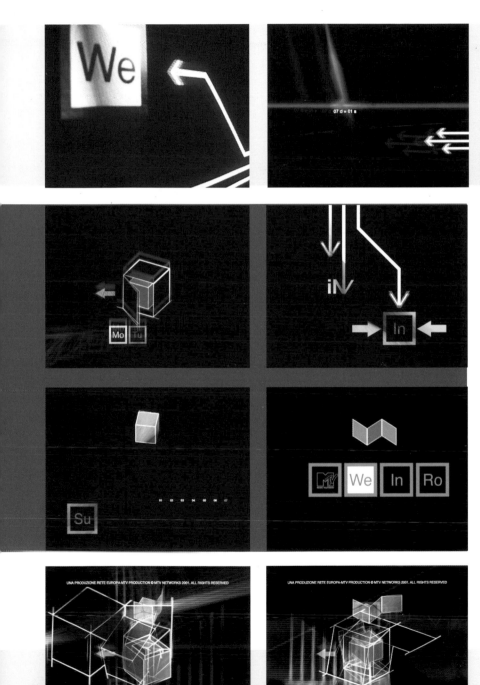
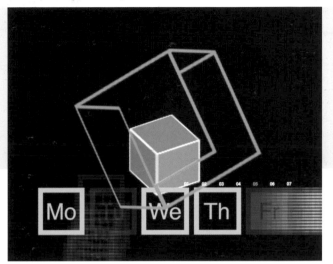

UNA PRODUZIONE RETE EUROPA-MTV PRODUCTION © MTV NETWORKS 2001. ALL RIGHTS RESERVED

UNA PRODUZIONE RETE EUROPA-MTV PRODUCTION © MTV NETWORKS 2001. ALL RIGHTS RESERVED

UNA PRODUZIONE RETE EUROPA-MTV PRODUCTION © MTV NETWORKS 2001. ALL RIGHTS RESERVED

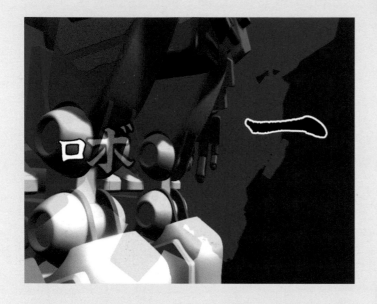

ロボ 一

ロボシト ロ

ボシン

SHIELD ACTIVATED

ボシン

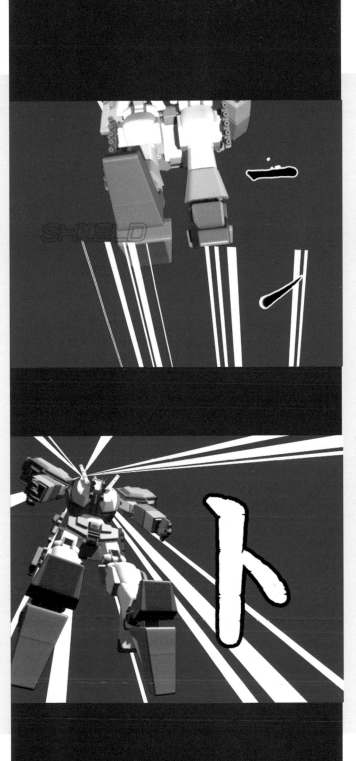

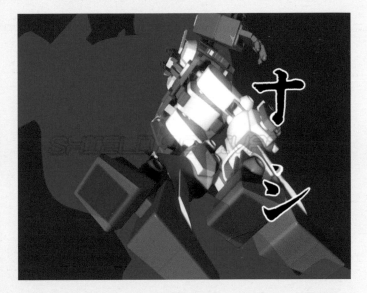

Robothon
MTV Italia
10''
2000

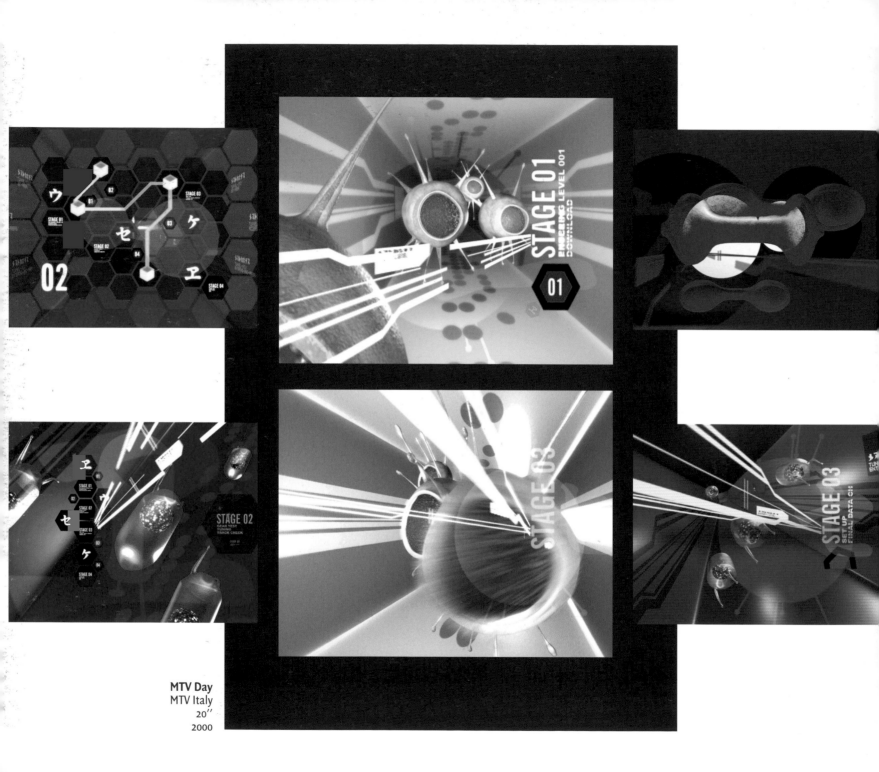

MTV Day
MTV Italy
20″
2000

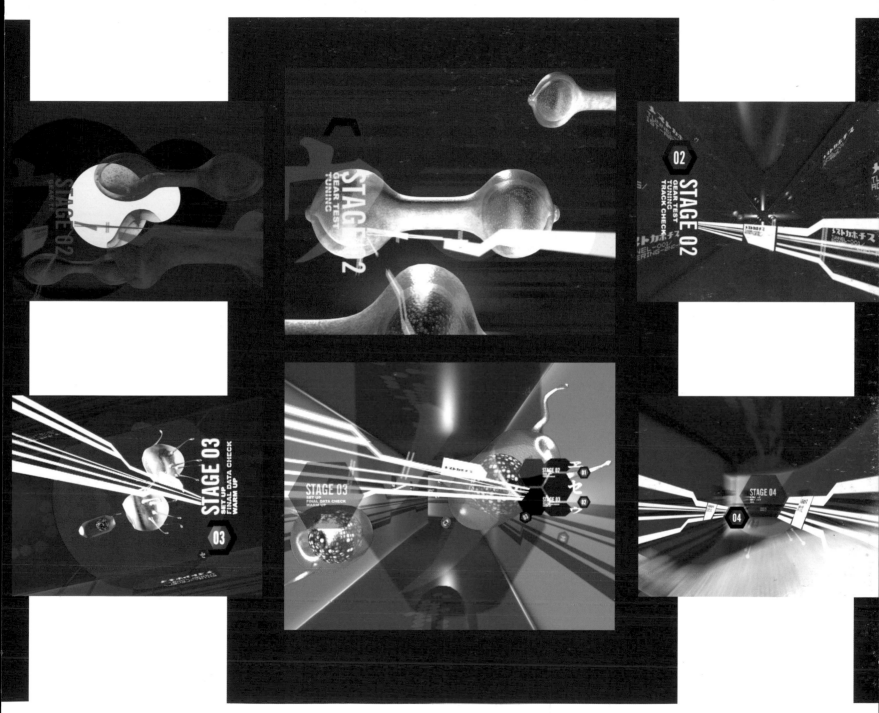

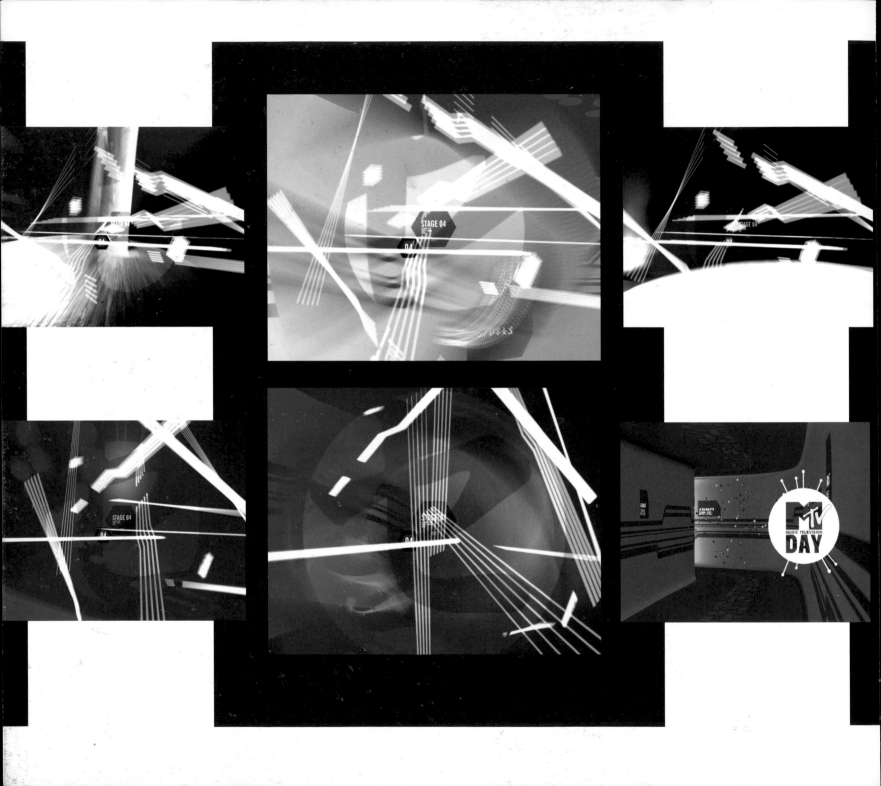

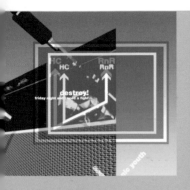

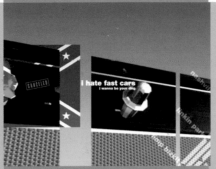

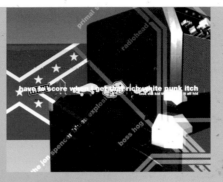

Channel Identity
(Hip-Hop/Rock 'N' Roll bumpers)
MTV Italy
5'' + 3''
2001

Select
MTV Spain
15''
2000

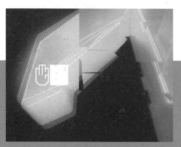
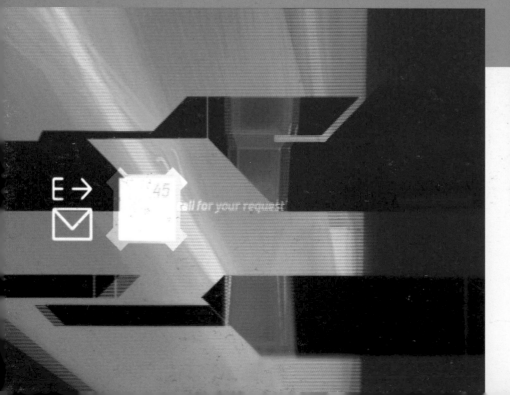
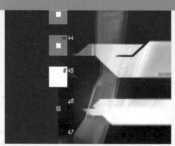
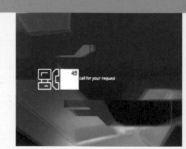

m 44

g 45
check the on-screen playlist

s 46

h 47

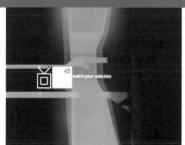

m 44

s 45

s 46

h 47

45 watch your selection

45 watch your selection

select MTV

FLORIA SIGISMONDI
L'ORRORE... L'ORRORE

Testi: *Matteo Bittanti*

"Il corpo in decadimento e' cio' che ognuno sente quando e' vivo"
(FLORIA SIGISMONDI)

Corpi amputati. Smembrati. Putrefatti. Deformi. Sfigurati. Grotteschi. Mutanti. *Mostri.*
Sigismondi – *come Chris Cunningham, piu' di Chris Cunningham* - mette in scena una corporeita' mostruosa. Una poetica che e' allo stesso tempo post-umana e anti-umana.
La produzione dell'artista canadese si colloca al punto di intersezione tra due culture profondamente differenti: quella classica – evidente nei suoi costanti riferimenti alla mitologia greca e alla tragedia – e quella post-moderna, contraddistinta dal rifiuto per l'armonia, il che si traduce, narrativamente, nel rifiuto per una diegesi tradizionale, innocua e lineare. Ne risulta un *maelstrom* di immagini deliranti dal quale emerge una fascinazione perversa per i mostri generati dal sonno della ragione. Come Medusa, Sigismondi possiede uno sguardo che impietrisce lo spettatore. Partorisce personaggi a meta' tra l'umano e il diabolico: angeli sterminatori, dittatori fascisti, anime tormentate, angosciate e angoscianti. Visioni bizzarre e raccapriccianti, simili a quelle del serial killer di *The Cell* (diretto, non a caso, da un altro grande regista di video musicali, **Tarsen Singh**). Immagini che corrodono le pupille.
Sigismondi sta a Marylin Manson come **Mills** sta ad Air e **Cunningham** ad Apex Twin: binomi i cui termini si

esaltano e si completano vicendevolmente. Il sodalizio tra l'artista canadese e il principe del gotico americano ha prodotto frutti dal sapore gustosamente rancido. Hubris e pathos, eros e thanatos. In the *Beautiful People* (1997), Manson e' una sorta di gerarca nazista circondato da demoni decaduti che si muove in uno scenario allucinante, popolato da vermi e apparecchi di tortura. Vasche come feretri, bulbi oculari che galleggiano nelle tazzine del caffe', protesi a meta' tra il meccanico e l'organico. Il gusto per il disgusto e' evidente anche nel secondo video di Manson, *Tourniquet*, nel quale il controverso artista si produce in una (in)dimenticabile depilazione dell'ascella. Il *modus operandi* sigismondiano prevede l'inserimento - spesso nel background - di un personaggio che si muove in modo disarticolato, inumano, come fosse in preda di un devastante attacco epilettico. La stessa tecnica usata da Lyne nel sottovalutato *Allucinazione Perversa*. Mostri, dicevamo: in *She Makes Me Wanna Die*, Tricky – il cui volto gia' di per se' inquietante viene ulteriormente deformato dal *make-up* – e' un demone dalla lingua biforcuta.

FLORIA SIGISMONDI
THE HORROR...THE HORROR

Text: *Matteo Bittanti*

"There's something interesting about being mortal and watching the body die"
(Floria Sigismondi)

Amputated. Dismembered. Putrefied. Rotten. Deformed. Disfigured. Grotesque. Mutated. You won't find a conventional anatomy in Sigismondi's world. Monsters. Only monsters. Sigismondi – like Chris Cunningham, more than Chris Cunningham – loves to display hideous flesh. Mutant creatures and physical rot, offset by porcelain-white fairies, cadavers and crumbling surfaces, fill her hallucinations. She possesses a post-human sensibility that it is also radically anti-human. The works of this Canadian artist lie at the intersection between two radically different cultures: a classical one – as it emerges in her constant references to Greek mythology and the great tragedies of Italian opera – and a post-modern one, marked by a refusal for harmony which is expressed in a narrative style that defies linearity. Her video work is characterized by a dramatic, provocative imagery. The atrocity exhibition. On the other side of the barricade, the viewer of Sigismondi's videos drowns in a *maelstrom* of delirious images characterized by a morbid fascination for monstrosity. Just like Medusa, Sigismondi's gaze can petrify those who dare to watch. She gives birth to half-man, half-diabolical creatures: exterminating angels, fascist dictators, tormented souls. It is the pure triumph of visual anguish. We are constantly presented with bizarre, disturbing visions similar to those produced by the mind of the serial killer we encountered in Tarsen Singh's feature film *The Cell* (incidentally, another music video director).

Images saturated with colors that corrode the retina. Sigismondi is to Marylin Manson what Cunningham is to Apex Twin: outrageous couples whose artistic sensibility is reciprocally stimulated. The perverted liaison between the Canadian artist and the prince of Goth has produced rancid fruits that carry hubris and pathos, Eros and Thanatos. In the *Beautiful People*'s (1997) clip, for instance Manson is a crazed fascist dictator hooked into a bizarre facial brace. As he moves in a rotting territory, where worms and torture instruments create a sick ambiance, we are presented a vast array of eyeballs floating in coffee cups, organic prostheses, fallen angels, and bath tubs used as coffins. The taste for disgust also emerges clearly in Manson's "Tourniquet". The clip is filled with antique mannequins and features a dancer with makeup flaking off her skin like old paint. One of the most memorable/forgettable images is the controversial artist shaving his shaving his pits and legs, and metamorphosing into an insect.

One of Sigismondi's trademarks consists in inserting a character – often in the background –that moves in an inhuman, disarticulate way, as if he were victim of a devastating epileptic attack. This is the same technique used by Lyne in the under rated *Jacob's Ladder* (1991).

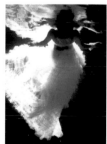

Nel video, Martina e' sdraiata in una vasca piena di serpenti. In un'altra scena, il suo volto e' coperto da un velo nero. Alla fine, la vediamo trasformata in un Medusa.

Mostri, dicevamo: In una sequenza del clip di *Dead Man Walking*, un Bowie caduto sulla terra, invecchiato, imbruttito, malato, sordo e cieco, grida il suo dolore straziante con la stessa intensita' dell'Urlo munchiano. *Little Wonder* e' una sorta di manichino post-espressionista che si muove in una New York da incubo, le cui stazioni della metropolitana sono infestate da creature grottesche.

Mostri visibili e invisibili, per parafrasare **Chuck Palaniuk**.

Al centro della riflessione sigismondiana troviamo la dimensione onirica, il gusto per il macabro, la morte e l'eccesso. L'elemento liquido – vasche da bagno, acqua, piscine - ricorre ossessivamente: e' il modo attraverso il quale Sigismondi, che ha rischiato di morire annegata in gioventu' , esorcizza il suo demone-trauma. Un altro *leit-motiv* e' la religione, riconducibile alla rigida educazione cattolica ricevuta. Nelle sue produzioni iconografiche compaiono crocifissi, martiri, suore e preti. Dall'unione delle categorie del sacro (rappresentata dalla madre cattolica) e del profano (il padre ateo) scaturisce un'estetica a meta' tra il blasfemo e il sadomaso. Sessualita' malata, perversa, patologica, quasi barkeriana. Nei video di Sigismondi confluiscono stili e soluzioni riconducibili ad artisti come **Francis Bacon**, Hans Belmer, **David Lynch**, Joel-Peter Wilkin, Tim Burton, Roman Polanski, David Cronenberg, Federico Fellini e Robert Wiene (*Il Gabinetto del Dr. Caligari*, 1919). Seguendo l'esempio di Dario Argento, la Sigismondi dorme poco: l'artista ha piu' volte dichiarato di privarsi volontariamente del sonno al fine di raggiungere uno stato mentale simile al nirvana.

Un nirvana da incubo.

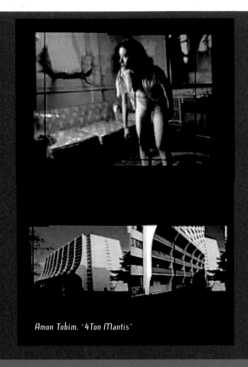

Amon Tobim, "4Ton Mantis"

Floria Sigismondi nasce a Pescara nel 1965 da una coppia di cantanti lirici, ma all'eta' di due anni lascia l'Europa per Hamilton, Canada. Studia disegno ed arti illustrative presso l'OCA (Ontario College of Art and Design) di Toronto. La passione per la fotografia la spinge ad abbandonare la tela per la pellicola. Ancora fresca di laurea, la ventiquattrenne Sigismondi si aggiudica il prestigioso National Magazine Award. Realizza copertine degli album di band alternative, pubblicita' per Coca Cola e Converse. Quindi, dietro richiesta Don Allan della casa di produzione Revolver Films, comincia a cimentarsi con video musicali. Realizza clip per gruppi canadesi come Pure, Victor, 13 Engines, Harem Scarem e The Tea Party (*Certain Saint of Light, Save Me, The River*). Rimane impressionato dal suo gusto per il gotico nientemeno che Marylin Manson, che le commissiona due video, The Beautiful People e Torniquet. Anche grazie alla splendida fotografia di Chris Soos, le sue creazioni ottengono immediatamente una serie di riconoscimenti. E' la consacrazione. Sigismondi lavora in seguito con artisti come Dawid Bowie, Barry Adamson, Tricky, Sheryl Crow, Plant e Page.

Nella seconda meta' degli anni novanta, si dedica anche alla pubblicita' e dirige una serie di spot per agenzie come TBWA/Chiat/Day, The Partners' Film Company (Canada) e British Believe Media (Stati Uniti). Tra i piu' celebri segnaliamo quelli per Shopper's Drug Mart (Opera Singer), Adidas (Cynics), 3DFX ed Eaton. In Cynics, il giocatore dei Lakers Kobe Bryant viene attaccato da orde di insetti di kafkiana memoria. Sigismondi incarna l'archetipo dell'artista completa: cantante di musica lirica, fotografa, scultrice, regista di video musicali e web designer. I suoi lavori sono stati esposti nelle gallerie piu' importanti del mondo, tra cui la John Gibson Gallery di Manhattan e Institute of Contemporary Arts di Londra. Nel settembre del 2000, la svolta digitale: Sigismondi "dirige" I've Seen it All di Björk, uno dei primi webeo (leggi: video interattivo) per il sito di MTV. A questo va ad aggiungersi la collaborazione con artisti come Amon Tobin e God Speed You Black Emperor, che si e' tradotta in produzioni video interamente digitali. L'artista canadese sta attualmente lavorando alla sceneggiatura di un film sulla Dalia Nera, le cui riprese cominceranno quest'anno. Floria Sigismondi vive tra New York e Toronto.

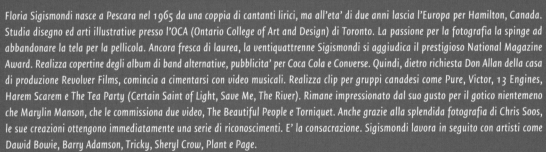

Essential **Videography**

Our Lady Peace, "The birdman"	1994
Marilyn Manson, "Tourniquet"	1996
Marilyn Manson, "Beautiful People"	1996
Catherine, "Four Leaf Clover"	1996
Pure, "Anna"	1996
Tricky, "She Makes Me Wanna Die"	1997
Fluffy, "Black Eye"	1997
David Bowie, "Dead Man Walking"	1997
David Bowie, "Little Wonder"	1997
Sarah McLachlan, "Sweet Surrender"	1998
Page and Plant, "Most High"	1998
Barry Adamson, "Can't Get Loose"	1999
Sheryl Crow, "Anything But Down"	1999
Amel Larrieux, "Get Up"	1999
Amon Tobim, "4 ton mantis"	1999

nota: Le immagini di queste pagine sono tratte dal libro Redemption (Die Gestalten Verlag ,1999)

note: The images of these pages were originally published in Redemption (Die Gestalten Verlag ,1999)

Monsters, we said. In "*She Makes Me Wanna Die*", Tricky – whose already daunting face is made even creepier by the make-up, an eerie combination of silent-era cinema paleness, expressionist art, baroque and war paint – is a demon with a bifurcating tongue. In the video, Martina lies in a bathtub replete with snakes. In another scene, a black veil covers her face. At the ends, she becomes a medusa. Monsters, we said. In "*Dead Man Walking*", we are presented with an aged, sick, deaf Bowie who fell to earth just to lament his excruciating pain. As Munch's paint, this image is not easy to forget. In "Little Wonder", Bowie wears a Ziggy Stardust-esque ensemble and acts like a post-expressionist mannequin. He wanders in a nightmarish New York, whose metro stations are infested by grotesque creatures. The usual eyeball appears in a teacup.

(in)visible monsters, to paraphrase Chuck Palaniuk.

Fatality, decay and physical deterioration have long haunted Sigismondi's psyche. Death and the macabre. The liquid element – bathtubs, water, pools – recurs obsessively in her works. It is as if the artist was trying to exorcize her childhood nightmares: as a young child, she nearly drowned a raft she was on capsized. A second leitmotiv is religion. Sigismondi's iconography consists of crucifixes, martyrs, nuns and priests. Her odd syncretism is the outcome of her contradictory religious background, which juxtaposes the sacred (i.e., her fervent Catholic mother), and the profane (i.e. her father was an atheist). Her ambiguous aesthetic sensibility is part blasphemy, part S&M. Add a sick, perverted, pathological, sexuality, the same sexuality that emerges in the tainted pages of Clive Barker's narrative. Sigismondi's videos are redolent of Francis Bacon, Hans Belmer, David Lynch, Joel-Peter Wilkin, Tim Burton, Roman Polanski, David Cronenberg, Federico Fellini, and Robert Wiene. Floria's predilection for plagued underworlds arises from her self-described "scandalous" subconscious. These nebulous realms are revealed to her in dreams, nightmares or in the meditative state of weary delirium that occurs between wakefulness and sleep. She often mentions that she deprives herself of rest in order to reach a Nirvana-like state of mind. Apparently, it works.

Born in Pescara, Italy in 1965, Floria, named after a character in the opera Tosca, left Europe at the age of two, when she moved to industrial town of Hamilton, Canada. She studied painting and illustration at the OCA (Ontario College of Art and Design) in Toronto. it was the two photography classes she took in her final years that sparked her creative fervor. She abandoned the brush for camera and pursued photography with persistent enthusiasm. She graduated with a stunning portfolio, racking up awards in the process. At the age of 24, she was granted the prestigious National Magazine Award for her unconventional works. Sigismondi also produced the cover art for alternative bands and began a career as a music video director. One of her most intriguing early works is the clip for Catherine's "Four Leaf Clover" which features the androgynous male singer stripping off several layers of panties. She also created avant-garde clips for Canadian bands like Pure, Victor, 13 Engines, The Tea Party, and Harem Scarem. The video she directed for Harem Scarem, which alludes to the German expressionist cult film The Cabinet of Dr. Caligari (1919) was caught by shock rocker Marylin Manson. Fascinated by her provocative and imaginative style, he asked her to create his videos. The results were The Beautiful People and Torniquet. Thanks to Chris Soos' stunning photography, Sigismondi's creations won a series of prizes. She then worked with blockbuster artists such as David Bowie, Barry Adamson, Tricky, Plant, Page and Sheryl Crow. In the second half of the Nineties, Sigismondi directed a series of TV commercials for TBWA/Chiat/Day, The Partners' Film Company (Canada) and British Believe Media (United States). Memorable spots are Shopper's Drug Mart (Opera Singer), Adidas (Cynics), 3DFX and Eaton. In Cynics, Lakers's player Kobe Bryant defends himself from a horde of Kafkaesque bugs. Sigismondi is the prototypical complete artist as she comprises comprised of a spectrum of artistic disciplines -- painting, sculpture, singing, design, photography and film. Her works have been exhibited in the most renowned galleries around the world, including John Gibson Gallery in Manhattan, New York and The London Institute of Contemporary Arts. The new millennium began with a digital switch for Sigismondi, as she "directed" Björk's I've Seen it All webeo, an interactive music video for MTV's website. She also collaborated with such artists as Amon Tobin and God Speed You Black Emperor. Sigismondi is currently working on her first feature, a full-length film on the Black Dalia.

Tricky, "Hell is round the corner"

Artista transalpino noto soprattutto per le sue suggestive fotografie, Stephane Sednaoui vanta una lunga serie di collaborazioni per le riviste piu' trendy del pianeta, da *The Face* ad *Arena*, senza dimenticare *Details*, *Vogue Hommes*, *Detours*, *Interview*, *Per Lui* e altre ancora. Sednaoui ha anche ricoperto una piccola parte – quella di un fotografo - nel terzo film di Gregg Araki, *Nowhere* (1997), che racconta la storia di un gruppo di alienati liceali losangelini. Sednaoui si cimenta con l'arte dei video musicali a partire dalla fine degli anni ottanta. Produce clip per artisti per lo piu' francesi come Shawn Christopher, El DeBarge, Eram, Naomi, High Five, Go West, Father MC, Suave, Smokey Robinson, Ex-Girlfriend, Alain Souchon. E' suo il video tratto dal catastrofico *Hudson Hawk* (1991), interpretato Dr. John & Bruce Willis. La sua sensibilita' artistica, unita ad una freschezza fuori dal comune, non passano inosservate e, all'inizio degli anni novanta, il tocco magico di Sednaoui finisce per impreziosire i lavori visuali di super star come **U2** ("Mysterious Ways"), **Madonna** ("Fever"), **R.E.M.** ("Lotus") e Alanis Morissette ("Ironic"). Oltre ai video, il nostro realizza copertine per icone pop del calibro di Madonna, Chic, Mick Jagger, Grace Jones e PM Dawn. La sua struggente e peculiare sensibilita' artistica gli hanno consentito di vincere l'MTV Award per il video piu' innovativo dell'anno nel 1992 con "Give it Away" (Red Hot Chili Peppers). Il clip, tecnicamente semplice ma caratterizzato da una straordinaria energia, mostra i membri della band, interamente ricoperti di vernice metallica, impegnati in un ballo spastico nel bel mezzo del deserto. I lavori di Sednaoui per **Bjork** non sono visivamente originali quanto quelli di Chris Cunningham, ma posseggono tuttavia un fascino particolare. E' difficile restare calmi ed indifferenti di fronte all'isteria contagiosa di "Big Time Sensuality" (1993), in cui la telecamera riprende l'irresistibile balletto di Bjork nelle vie di New York. Sednaoui sembra inoltre essere ossessionato dall'idea che la realta' non e' mai quella che appare, come nel famoso aforisma di Gilbot e Sullivan tanto caro a Philip K. Dick ("*Le cose non sono mai quello che sembrano/Il latte magro si maschera da crema*"). Ad esempio, nel video "The Chemicals Between Us" per Bush, tratto dall'album *The Science Of Things*, il regista gioca con il concetto degli universi paralleli. Il video alterna scene della band che suona in una strada desolata e senza vita, e altre tratte da una dimensione alternativa, bianco, pieno di geishe, bambini, monaci Shaolin e giardini giapponesi. Allo stesso modo, nel video di "Sly", per **Massive Attack**, il contrasto e' tra la frenesia della citta' e la tranquillita' del giardino, tra materialismo e leggerezza buddista. In questo psichedelico ed iper-realista video, i membri della band passano da una scena all'altra provoncando vere e proprie esplosioni di colori che finiscono per contaminare l'asettico scenario metropolitano. E' tuttavia nei video realizzati per **Tricky** che il talento di Sednaoui emerge in modo dirompente. "Hell's around the corner", che debutta nell'agosto del 1995, e' un trip schizoide ma al tempo stesso ipnotico dominato da cromatismi magenta, un riflessione cinematica sulla follia e sulla insostenibile leggerezza dell'essere ("*Lobotomy ensures my good behavior/The constant struggle ensures my insanity*").

STÉPHANE SEDNAOUI
VIVE LA FRANCE!

Testi: *Matteo Bittanti*

Madonna, "Fever"

Bjork, "Big Time Sensuality"

STÉPHANE SEDNAOUI
VIVE LA FRANCE!

Text: Matteo Bittanti

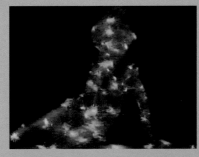

Tricky, "Pumpkin"

Stephane Sednaoui is a French artist who is primarily known for his photographic efforts. His works have appeared on hip magazines such as *The Face, Arena, Details, Vogue Hommes, Detours, Interview, Per Lui* and many others. Sednaoui has also played a minor role – incidentally, a photographer - in Gregg Araki's third feature, *Nowhere* (1997), which tells the story of a group of spoiled high school kids living in Los Angeles. Sednaoui first foray on the music video scene goes back to the late 8os, when he started producing clips for (mostly) French artists such as Shawn Christopher, El DeBarge, Eram, Naomi, High Five, Go West, Father MC, Suave, Smokey Robinson, Ex-Girlfriend, Alain Souchon. He has even directed the video of catastrophic movie *Hudson Hawk*, which starred Dr. John & Bruce Willis. His artistic sensibility combined with an unusual freshness did not go unnoticed and, by the early Nineties, Sednaoui was working with some of the biggest stars in the music industry. Meanwhile, he also produced the cover art for pop icons such as Madonna, Chic, Mick Jagger, Grace Jones, and PM Dawn. Sednaoui has directed an insane amount of music videos for performers like U2 ("Mysterious Ways"), Madonna ("Fever"), R.E.M. ("Lotus"), and Alanis Morissette ("Ironic"). His staggering and unique artistic sensibility led him to win the MTV's Best Breakthrough Video Award in 1992 for the Red Hot Chili Peppers' "Give it Away", which showcased the members of the band, covered with metallic paint, spastically dancing in the desert. A very simplistic but powerful video. Sednaoui's works for **Bjork** are visually not as inventive as Cunningham's, yet equally fascinating. "Big Time Sensuality" (1993), for instance, is an irresistible, hysterical romp through the streets of New York. Sednaoui seems to be obsessed with the idea that reality is never what is seems, as in that famous Gilbot's and Sullivan's aphorism ("*Things are seldom what they seem/Skim milk masquerades as cream*"). In Bush's video for "The Chemicals Between Us," the first single from the album *The Science Of Things*, the director toys with the concept of parallel universes, one in which the band is playing on a bleak and desolate street, and a hyperreal, sallow space replete with geishas, children, Shaolin monks, and Japanese gardens. Similarly, in **Massive Attack**'s "Sly", the contrast is between the city and the garden. In this psychedelic video, the members of the band endlessly transfer from a context to the other, as a variety of colors explode behind them. His outstanding talent, however, can be fully appreciated only in Tricky's clips. "Hell's around the corner", which debuted in August 1995, is a schizophrenic yet mesmerizing trip dominated by magenta chromatic tones, a cinematic reflection on madness and the unbearable lightness of being ("*Lobotomy ensures my good behavior/The constant struggle ensures my insanity*"). The camera follows **Tricky**, who is, just for a change, deliriously mumbling. At one point, the artist - who is wearing a bright red T-shirt and bizarre make-up on his face – experiences some sort of demonic transformation and his head morphs into Martina's. The bizarre video ends with an increasingly unstable Tricky melting with the red background. The follow-up, "Pumpkin", which was lunched a month later, is dominated by the color blue. In this video, **Allison Goldfrapp**, who is singing melancholically in the street, has replaced Martina. A red light, much like a laser, is pointing at the artists' faces as they sing. As the video progresses, mysterious figures carrying flash lights materialize from both sides of the streets and approach them in a sinister, paranoid manner (see Bradbury's magnificent short-story, *The Crowd*). It is a rotten radiance that blinds, much like William Gibson's *Virtual Light* ("*I can't breathe and I can't see… And it feels like I must be blind*"). The themes of alienation, isolation and hostility are reinforced by "Here Come The Aliens" (February 1996), which was actually made more than a year before the song appeared on the "Makes Me Wanna Die" single and the arrangements are slightly different. Blue and red are gone, replaced by a more solemn black and white. The video stars Tricky, Martina, and Afrika Izlam. We follow them as they ride on the metro, which clearly symbolizes the subconscious. Sitting on the train, they go through tunnels, accompanied by the stream-of-consciousness of the lyrics. The images are often blurred and the camera fades in and out of them. The lack of focus reflects our

Bjork, "Possibly maybe"

La macchina da presa segue/perseguita Tricky che, tanto per cambiare, e' perso in un rosario di incomprensibili deliri. Ad un certo punto, l'artista, che indossa una maglietta rossa e strati abbondanti di trucco sul volto – e' vittima di una sorta di demoniaca trasformazione. Con un effetto di *morphing*, Tricky diventa Martina (o e' il contrario?). Il video si conclude con l'assorbimento del sempre piu' instabile Tricky ("*My brain thinks bomb-like, bomb-like*") nel fondale rosso sangue. Il seguito, "Pumpkin", apparso un mese dopo e sempre tratto da *Maxinquaye*, e' invece dominato da cromatismi blu. Qui Martina e' stata rimpiazzata da Allison Goldfrapp, che sola se ne va per le vie della citta' esoricizzando tutta la sua melanconia. Una luce rossa, simile ad un laser, illumina il volto dei cantanti. Man mano che il video prosegue, misteriosi personaggi equipaggiati con torce elettriche si materializzano nelle strade e si avvicinano a Tricky ed Allison in modo inquietante (come la folla dell'omonimo, magnifico racconto di Ray Bradbury). Il video e' pervaso da una luce marcia che, come quella *virtuale* di William Gibson, acceca anziche' illuminare ("*I can't breathe and I can't see... And it feels like I must be blind*"). I temi ricorrenti – alienazione, isolamento, ostilita' – ritornano anche in "Here Come The Aliens" (febbraio 1996), prodotto piu' di un anno prima che il brano venisse pubblicato insieme al singolo "Makes Me Wanna Die" e presenta arrangiamenti leggermente differenti. Il rosso ed il blu sono evaporati. Qui dominano bianco e nero. Il video, interpretato da Tricky, Martina e Afrika Izlam, si svolge in larga parte nella metropolitana, chiara metafora del subsconscio. Seduti sul treno, i tre percorrono tunnel interminabili mentre risuonano liriche formattate secondo lo *stream-of-consciousness*. Le immagini sono spesso sfuocate e la macchina da presa ondeggia nervosamente. La mancanza di messa a fuoco riflette chiaramente la crescente incapacita' dei personaggi di distinguere tra realta' e fantasia, veglia e sonno. Le immagini sono talvolta filtrate dal vetro del treno: incapaci di trovare il senso delle cose nelle cose stesse (Husserl), ci affacciamo disperati da altre "finestre", dai mille schermi della televisione e dei computer. Come in *Allucinazione Perversa* (1991), questo e' un viaggio di sola andata, la cui ultima fermata e' l'inferno. *Biglietti, prego*. Spazio e tempo sono compressi, estesi ed accelerati: vediamo solo per un istante degli incompresibili graffiti, luci lampeggianti, poi la corsa rallenta, quindi accelera di nuovo, quindi rallenta di nuovo. Ancora piu' criptico e' "For Real" (1999), il primo video tratto dall'album *Juxtapose*. Qui Tricky e' seduto su un tavolo di un ristorante orientale. Il movimento circolare della camera attorno al tavolo mostra clienti sempre diversi. Tricky blatera parole sensa senso, a volte a se stesso, altre volte ai suoi apatici vicini ("*It's not real/It's just passed the time*"). Poco dopo lascia il ristorante e si avvia verso un barbiere. Seduto nel negozio con un asciugamani sul volto, Tricky resta solo, a fissare la sua immagine riflessa nello specchio, oggetto/icona che ritroviamo anche nel bellissimo video di MC Solaar, "Le Nouveau Western". Nel video, l'interazione tra Tricky e gli altri personaggi e' pressoche' inesistente. "For Real" esplora i temi della solitudine e della incomunicabilita'.

Siamo soli, *per davvero*.

inability to distinguish between reality and fantasy. Sometimes we just see the picture through the window of the metro just like we try to make sense of reality through the mediation of countless other windows, e.g. television screens and computer monitors. As in *Jacob's Ladder* (Adrian Lyne, 1991), this is a one-way ride whose final destination is hell. *Tickets, please*. Time and space are deflated, inflated, compressed, and accelerated: we get a glimpse of incomprehensible graffiti, blinking lights, as the train goes slower, than faster, than slower again. Even more cryptic is "For Real" (1999), the first video from the album *Juxtapose*. Here, Tricky is sitting on a large table in a dining room of an Asian restaurant. As the camera circumnavigates the table, we realize that the guests change constantly. Tricky is mouthing the lyrics, partly to himself, party to his aphasic neighbors. Afterward, he leaves the restaurant and walks in a barbershop. Someone puts a towel on his face and he is left all alone, looking at his reflection in the mirror (an object that is also heavily featured in the video for MC Solaar's "Le Nouveau Western"), still singing the lyrics. In this video, the interaction between Tricky and the other characters is practically non-existing. "For Real" is about loneliness and lack of communication. We're alone, *for real*.

Essential **Video**graphy

JONATHAN GLAZER
IL GLASSIFICATORE

Testi: Matteo Bittanti

Glazer: s.m., colui che applica smalto o glassa a una superficie di ceramica, vetro o porcellana.

Jonathan Glazer, professione smaltatore.
Prezzi modici. Telefonare per appuntamento.

Jonathan Glazer e' uno smaltatore professionista. Glazer tuttavia non lavora con ceramica, vetro o porcellana. Glazer smalta immagini. Ricopre la pellicola con un sottile velo di glassa. Crea immagini appiccicose, che si attaccano al cervello, alle dita. Immagini che macchiano. Che lasciano il segno. Immagini eccessive, che provocano la nausea. Immagini che trasudano karma. Immagini in coma. Immagini cosi' schoccanti che ti verrebbe voglia di chiamare la polizia. Materializzatosi in Inghilterra nel 1966, Jonathan Glazer si laurea in arti teatrali presso il Polytechnic College del Middlesex, ma, seguendo l'esempio di Ridley Scott, si lascia presto ammaliare dalla sirena della pubblicita' e dei video. Il suo debutto - e che debutto! - risale al 1995 con "Karmacoma" per **Massive Attack**. Esplicito *homage* a *The Shining* di **Stanley Kubrick**, il video e' un *collage* di atmosfere surreali ed oniriche. Mentre **Tricky** balbetta parole prive senso [*"Walking through the suburbs though not exactly lovers/You're a couple, 'specially when your body's doubled/Duplicate, then you wait for the next Kuwait"*], l'occhio passeggia su e giu' per le stanze dell'Overlook versione due punto zero, si riposa e assaggia il resto [*Take a walk take a rest taste the rest*]. Sogni che diventano incubi, come in **Bunuel**. L'influenza del maestro Kubrick – se non altro a livello stilistico - e' evidente anche in "Karma Police" (1997), straordinario clip per Radiohead, un lungo piano sequenza che lascia senza fiato. **Thom Yorke** abulico apatico catatonico – occhi chiusi, *non guardare, non vedere, sogna piuttosto* – giace nel sedile posteriore di un'auto, che parte all'inseguimento di un uomo [*I've Given All I Can*]. Ad un certo punto l'uomo in fuga si ferma si gira si volta fronteggia i suoi inseguitori scorge un rivolo di benzina sull'asfalto sogghigna satanicamente estrae l'accendino gli da' fuoco l'auto fa retromarcia ma le fiamme corrono corrono piu' velocemente e in un attimo la raggiungono

[*It's Not Enough*]. Thom non c'e' piu', e' sparito. Fuoco cammina con me. "Karma Police" e' video straordinariamente lynchiano, ellittico, *tres lost highway*, inseguimenti nella notte, strade che non portano da nessuna parte perche' il punto di partenza e' anche il punto di arrivo. La fonte di ispirazione di "Karma Police", ha confessato Glaser, e' un incubo che lo ha tormentato per anni. L'inseguitore che diventa inseguito, la vittima carnefice. Immagini che si accompagnano perfettamente alle liriche, o e' il contrario? Thom cieco, Thom come Tiresia, Thom che narra la storia, ma il vero protagonista e' lo spettatore, dietro il volante. E' lo spettatore che alla fine viene arso vivo. Il fuoco purifica lo sguardo.

Del resto, analoghe, propedeutiche tematiche le avevamo incontrate in "Street Spirit" (1996), sempre per **Radiohead**. La scena si svolge nel deserto alle porte di Los Angeles. Thom Yorke canta – ancora una volta i suoi occhi sono (soc)chiusi – mentre immagini apparentemente casuali, scorrono sul video e si accompagnano allo *stream of consciousness*. Cani che abbaiano, ragazzini, locuste, vernice, vetri rotti...
Nel frattempo, gli altri membri della band saltano su e' giu' dalle sedie. "Movimento" perpetuo, ma illusorio, perche' non c'e' un vero e proprio "spostamento".
Lo *slow motion* enfatizza, prolunga, dilata tempi e spazi. Il video vive nella dimensione fantastica dello spettatore prima ancora che sulla finestra dello schermo. Glazer aumenta le dosi di glassa per Jamiroquai, per il quale realizza video piu' accessibili e meno controversi. Tutt'altro che sorprendentemente, "Virtual Insanity" si aggiudica l'*MTV Video Award* nel 1997 nella categoria *Best Video of the Year*. Jay Kay recita il suo inno luddita ed antitechnologico in una

Massive Attack: Karmacoma

Blur: the original

JONATHAN GLAZER
THE GLAZIER

Text: Matteo Bittanti

Glazing: n. 1. A thin, smooth, shiny coating. 2. To apply a glaze to, like syrup on a doughnut. 3. To give a smooth, lustrous surface to. 4. A glassy film, as over the eyes.

Jonathan Glazer, professional glazier. Reasonable prices. For an appointment, please call during office hours.

Jonathan is a professional glazier. He does not deal with ceramics, glass or porcelain. He is only concerned with images. He applies a thin, smooth, shiny coating on the film. He creates sticky pictures that get stuck into the brain's cells. Images that leave stains behind them. Images that leave a mark. Excessive images, images that might cause nausea, queasiness and diarrhea. Images that perspire karma. Images that make you fall into a coma. Images so shocking that one is tempted to call the police. Glazer materialized in the U.K. in 1966. He graduated in theater design and direction in England in the 1980s and began his career as a freelance director working in the theater. But he soon switched to film and TV production and joined a company specialized in video trailers and promos. He teamed up with producer Nick Morris at Academy Commercials and, in just a couple of years, he was creating a variety of TV promos and short features, such as "Mad", Commission" and "Pool". At this point he moved into music videos. His groundbreaking debut, "Karmacoma" (1995), is an explicit homage to **Stanley Kubrick**'s *The Shining*, a collage of surreal, oniric images. As Tricky is gibbering meaningless lines ["*Walking through the suburbs though not exactly lovers/You're a couple, 'specially when your body's doubled/Duplicate, then you wait for the next Kuwait*"], the eye takes a walk through the rooms of what looks like version 2.0 of the Overlook Hotel, rests for a while and then tastes what is left ["*Take a walk take a rest taste the rest*"]. Dreams that become nightmares. Bunuel *docet*. The influence of Kubrick's – at least on a stylistic level – is also evident in another staggering video, "Karma Police" (1997) for **Radiohead**. It starts with a long, continuous shot that leaves the audience breathless. An abulic, catatonic Thom Yorke - *keep your eyes close, don't look, don't watch, dream instead* – lies in the back seat of a car chasing a desperate man [*I've Given All I Can*]. At one point, the running man stops, turns, faces his persecutors, falls to his knees from exhaustion but then realizes that the car is dripping gasoline, *oh yeah*, sweet, and he satanically grins, and takes his lighter out, and sets the trail of gas on fire, *fast faster*,

the car is now moving backward but the fire is *fast faster*, and it is just a matter of seconds before the car bursts into flames [*It's Not Enough*]. Thom has vanished. Vanished and gone. [*I've Given All I Can*]. Things will catch up with you, you know. Besides, fire walks with me. Disturbing references. You could say that David Lynch's *Lost Highway*, with his hypnotic chases in the night, elliptical narrative, roads that lead to nowhere because the points of departure and destination coincide, is a two hour long "Karma Police". But according to Glazer, the source of inspiration of this video was a nightmare that tormented him for years. The chaser that becomes the chased, the prey turns into the hunter [*But We're Still On The Payroll*]. Images that perfectly suit the lyrics, or is it the opposite? Thom is blind, Thom is a modern Tiresias, Thom is the narrator, but the real protagonist of the story is the viewer, who sits behind the wheel. Thom sits quietly in the back seat [a red-seat]. The viewer is the one burning in the end. Fire purifies the gaze. After all, we previously encountered similar themes in "Street Spirit" (1996), another elegant video for Radiohead. The clip, shot in black and white, takes place in a desert just outside of L.A. Thom is singing – once again, his eyes closed – while apparently random images flow onscreen and merge with the stream of consciousness. Barking dogs, kids, crickets, paint, broken glass... Meanwhile, the other members of the band jump from off chairs and other objects. Perpetual "movement"? No, it is just an illusion: believe me, nobody really gets anywhere. The repetitive slow motion shots emphasize/prolong/deflate time. The video lives in the chaotic dimension of the viewers' minds even before it becomes visible on the TV window. "Street Spirit" won the award for Best Pop Video and a special director's award at Music Week in 1996 [according to some, there is an alternate version which

Radiohead: Street Spirit

Radiohead: Karmapolice

Radiohead: Rabbit in your headlights

stanza dal design futuristico, vuota, blu e bianca. Il pavimento di muove come un *tapis roulant*, il mobilio appare e scompare, le pareti si allargano e si restringono. Niente silicio, per carita'! Siamo dalle parti di Melies, trucchi e barbatrucchi straordinariamente "analogici" e atecnologici: il set si muove per mezzo di ruote e le scene vengono riprese da una telecamera appesa al muro. L'illusione ottica e' convincente. E anche qui il protagonista del video si "*muove, ma non arriva da nessuna parte*" (non a caso, il titolo dell'album di Jamiroquai e' *Travelling Without Moving*). Un video incredibilmente semplice eppure affascinante, che non richiede la lettura di Metz e delle sue teorie sul *trucage* per poter essere apprezzato fino in fondo. Un video che non provoca le vertigini, non violenta l'occhio, ma lo seduce e lo veste in Stussy. Di tutt'altra pasta lo straordinario *Rabbit in Your Headlights* di **U.N.K.L.E.**), il capolavoro di Glazer. Un barbone che farnetica. Farnetica qualcosa mentre cammina nel tunnel [*un tunnel di Stoccolma*]. Farnetica qualcosa mentre gli automobilisti lo sfiorano, lo deridono, lo invitano a bordo [*ma lui non sale*]. Farnetica qualcosa mentre lo investono. Farnetica qualcosa mentre si rialza. Farnetica [*come Ellen Burstyn in Requiem for a Dream*]. Poi ad un certo punto, si ferma, allarga le braccia, come Gesu' Cristo crocifisso. [*I'm a rabbit in your headlights. Christian suburbaniteWashed down the toilet. Money to burn*] Un'altra auto lo prende in pieno, ma questa volta l'uomo non cade. L'auto invece esplode. Fine. Un video troppo controverso e sovversivo per la sempre piu' *mainstream* MTV, che si rifiuta di mandarlo in onda, dirottandolo su MTV2. C'e' molto di Adrian Lyne (*Allucinazione Perversa*), tanto nelle liriche di Yorke [*If you're frightened of dyin' and you're holding on... You'll see devils tearing your life away. But...if you've made your peace, Then the devila are really angels Freeing you from the earth.....from the earth....from the earth*] quanto nelle immagini di Glazer... Jonathan Glazer, smaltatore professionista. Glazer crea immagini appiccicose, che si attaccano al cervello, alle dita. Immagini che macchiano. Che lasciano il segno. Immagini eccessive, che provocano la nausea. Immagini che trasudano karma. Immagini in coma. Immagini cosi' shoccanti che ti verrebbe voglia di chiamare la polizia.

features a "coin flipping" shot with Johnny ending up being excluded] Glazer applied even more glaze in Jamiroquai's "Virtual Insanity", one of his most accessible videos. Rather unsurprisingly, it won the *MTV Award* for the *Best Video of the Year* (1997). Jay Kay recites his luddite-anthem in a futuristic-looking room. The floor moves as a *tapis roulant*, pieces of furniture appear and disappear (*now you see'em, now you don't*); the white walls enlarge and shrink. But there is no digital trickery here: it is all very rudimental, in the spirit of Melies'. The *trucage* is extraordinarily ordinary, anal-logical and a-technological. Jay moves, but never goes anywhere (incidentally, the album is titled *Travelling Without Moving*). The result? "Virtual Insanity" is a simple yet fascinating cinematic experience. It does not make the viewer feeling dizzy, does not rape his eyes, instead it seduces him and dresses him up in stussy. The video won Best Overall Video at the MVPA and Billboards Music Awards and got an unprecedented ten nominations for the 1997 **MTV Video Awards**, where it won Best Video, Best Cinematography, Best Special Effects, and Best Breakthrough Video.

U.N.K.L.E.'s *Rabbit in Your Headlights* is a totally different ballgame. To make a long story short, it is Glazer's masterpiece. A man is walking and raving. He is raving in the tunnel (a Stockholm tunnel). As he raves, cars get closer and closer, they even hit him, go figure. He raves as they run over him. He raves as he gets up as nothing happened. He raves, just like Ellen Burstyn in *Requiem for a Dream* after one too many pill. Then, at one point, he stops, spreads his arms in a Christ-like gesture [*I'm a rabbit in your headlights. Christian suburbanite/Washed down the toilet/. Money to burn*]. He is hit by another car, but this time he does not collapse. He does not break into pieces. This is not Leftield's *Afrika Shok* (Made in Cunningham). No way, he stands up. The car explodes. He raves. End of story. *Rabbit in Your Headlights* is too controversial and subversive for MTV US [luckily, **MTV2** took good care of it]. Yorke's lyrics create space in the viewer's imagination to complement the stream of consciousness. The song itself resembles the plot of Lyne's *Jacob's Ladder* (mental note: "Is this the quintessential movie of the Nineties?"): "*If you're frightened of dyin' and you're holding on... You'll see devils tearing your life away. But... if you've made your peace, Then the devils are really angels Freeing you from the earth... from the earth... from the earth.*" Jonathan is a professional glazier. But he does not deal with ceramics, glass or porcelain. His only concern is images. He applies a thin, smooth, shiny coating on the film. He creates sticky pictures that get stuck into the brain's cells. Images that leave stains. Images that leave a mark. Excessive images, that might cause nausea, queasiness and diarrhea. Images that perspire karma. Images that make you fall into a coma. Images so shocking that one is tempted to call the police.

MUSICA INTERATTIVA E SCENA POP GIAPPONESE: L'ASCESA/DISCESA DEI RHYTHM E MUSIC VIDEO GAMES

Testo: Matteo Bittanti
Immagini: Simone Crosignani

L'inarrestabile successo dei *rhythm and music games* – noti anche come *beat games* o *dance games* - rappresenta uno dei fenomeni socioludici più affascinanti degli ultimi anni. Al pari del pervasivo Pokemon – altro paradigmatico esempio della crescente mercificazione dell'immaginario collettivo – i *dance games* non potevano che spopolare in un paese, il Giappone, dove kitsch, disco music e tecnologia coesistono con sorprendente *nonchalance*. Più di una semplice moda, i *dance games* sono una ossessione nazionale che ha contagiato tanto gli otaku quanto i giocatori occasionali. Come si spiega tale successo? Le ragioni sono numerose. Facili da giocare, ma quasi impossibili da terminare, i *dance games* possono essere fruiti da chiunque, in modalità singola quanto collettiva. Presentano contenuti non-violenti e sono dunque adatti anche ad un pubblico infantile. E, cosa rara per un videogame, sono divertenti da vedere e non solo da giocare. Alcuni richiedono controller speciali, come pedaliere, piatti, chitarre elettroniche e persino maracas. Tutti sono caratterizzati da una componente grafica di grande impatto visuale e da soundtrack irresistibili.

The Last Days of Game Music

Punto di incontro tra videogiochi e musica elettronica, i *dance games* costituiscono ormai una fetta significativa del mercato. Basti pensare che quasi un quinto dei video games prodotti in Giappone nel 2000 appartenevano a questa categoria. Lentamente, ma inesorabilmente, l'influenza dei *dance games* si sta estendendo all'occidente. Un vero e proprio ritorno al futuro, dato che le radici del fenomeno possono essere rintracciate proprio negli Stati Uniti. Il progenitore è infatti *Simon*, un gioco elettronico creato da Ralph Baer, patriarca dei videogiochi nonchè inventore della prima console, Magnavox Odissey (1972). Prendendo spunto da un oscuro coin-op Atari, *Touch Me* (1974), nel quale il giocatore doveva ripetere in modo corretto una sequenza di luci emesse in modo casuale dal computer, Baer aveva creato una nuova versione nella quale alle luci lampeggianti era associata una sequenza di suoni elettronici. La variante di Baer piace a Milton Bradley che acquista il brevetto e lo produce su larga scala. Il risultato è *Simon* (1977), un *board-game* che diventa presto un *best-seller* internazionale ed inaugura la stagione dei giochi elettronici portatili.

Qualche anno più tardi, l'americana Epyx pubblica *Break Dance* (1984), un videogioco per Commodore 64 nel quale i giocatori dovevano copiare le mosse di snodabilissimi ballerini virtuali. È stata tuttavia Nintendo, nel 1988, a porre le basi del dance game moderno con l'introduzione del Power Pad, un tappetino dotato di sensori per NES che consentiva al giocatore di interagire con i personaggi sullo schermo attraverso i piedi anzichè con le mani. Uno dei pochi titoli pubblicati per la costosa espansione è *Dance Aerobics*, simulazione elettronica dell'omonimo ballo.

Dopo una decade di alti e bassi (molti bassi), il genere ha conosciuto una vera e propria esplosione nella seconda metà degli anni novanta. Fattori come l'avvento del CD come supporto comune ludico e musicale, l'apparizione di console dotate di processori sonori sempre più sofisticati combinata all'imprevedibile fantasia dei game designer nipponici hanno trasformato un passatempo per pochi nel karaoke del ventunesimo secolo.

Nobody beats Lammy when she's on the guitar!

UM JAMMER LEMMY

Text: *Matteo Bittanti*
Photos: *Simone Crosignani*

INTERACTIVE MUSIC AND THE JAPANESE POP SCENE: THE RISE/DEMISE OF RHYTHM AND MUSIC VIDEO GAMES

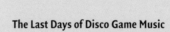

The overwhelming success of *rhythm and music games*, also known as *beat games* or *dance games*, represents one of the most fascinating socio-ludic phenomena in recent years. As the pervasive Pokemon – another paradigmatic example of the increasing commodification of the collective imaginary – the dance games craze could not take place anywhere but in Japan, a nation where kitsch, disco music and technology coexist with disarming casualness. More than a simple fad, *dance games* have become a national obsession, a highly contagious epidemic that spread among otakus as well casual players. The reasons behind this staggering success are diverse. For starters, the immediate appeal of these games, in which music and rhythm constitute an integral part of the gameplay, is easy to grasp. Moreover, they nearly all share the same fundamental principles: they're simple to play, easy to comprehend, yet virtually impossible to master. They can be played by almost anyone, either in single or collective modes. They contain a non-violent content and are therefore suitable to infantile audiences. Moreover, they are fun to watch as well as to play. After all, "people are the ultimate spectacle." Some of them require special interfaces, such as turntables, guitars, drums and even maracas. All are characterized by impressive visuals and irresistible soundtracks.

The Last Days of Disco Game Music

This new hybrid genre - part videogame, part electronic music, 100% pure unadulterated fun – constitutes a significant part of the Japanese gamescape. As a matter of fact, almost one fifth of all Japanese videogames produced in 2000 belonged to this category. Slowly, but inexorably, their influence is reaching the Western world. In a sense, it is a comeback, since dance gaming roots can be traced in the United States, where videogames themselves appeared in the first place. The ancestor is *Simon* (1977), an electronic game invented by Ralph Baer, the "patriarch" of videogames and creator of the first console, Magnavox's Odyssey (1972). Inspired by a rather obscure Atari's coin-op, *Touch Me* (1974), in which the player had to properly repeat a random-generated sequence of lights, Baer created an improved version that also featured sounds. Milton Bradley liked Baer's variant, bought the patent and produced it for the masses. *Simon* not only became a one of the most sought after game of the late Seventies but also

Parappa e i suoi fratelli

Il padre dei *dance games* è Masaya Matsuura. Nato nel giugno del 1961 a Osaka e laureatosi in Sociologia Industriale presso l'Università di Ritsumeikan, all'età di 19 anni Matsuura si innamora della musica elettronica. Scopre Apple II e un programma chiamato *Kaleidoscope* e la sua vita cambia radicalmente. Dopo dieci anni di esperienza nell'industria musicale – maturate con la band *PYSYS* (pronuncia "size") che ha debuttato nel 1983 con il singolo "Different View" - Matsuura si è dedicato alla musica interattiva, creando, all'inizio degli anni novanta un CD-ROM per Macintosh intitolato *The Seven Colors*, seguito dall'altrettanto brillante *X-Tool*. Ma il vulcanico *game designer*, leader maximo dello studio Na-Na-Oh-Sha, è diventato celebre a livello planetario grazie a *Parappa The Rappa* (PlayStation, 1996).

Un gameplay caratterizzato dalla pressione ritmica dei tasti alle liriche, unito ad uno stile grafico che riprende da un lato la *street culture*, dall'altra le illustrazioni dei libri per bambini, hanno reso *Parappa The Rappa* un vero e proprio cult. Figlio della globalizzazione del divertimento, il gioco PlayStation si pone al crocevia tra Occidente ed Oriente. Parappa è un cagnolino rapper esperto di arti marziali, follemente innamorato di un fiore parlante, Sunny Funny. I personaggi, creati dal disegnatore californiano Rodney Alan Greenblat, non occultano la loro natura bidimensionale dietro ad ammassi di poligoni. Al contrario, si piegano come se fossero fatti di carta - non a caso Parappa significa "piatto", "sottile come un foglio" - e danzano spensieratamente in scenari surreali. *Parappa The Rappa* è permeato da uno humor assolutamente demenziale, dalle liriche che ti restano appiccicate al cervello ("*Don't get cocky/It's gonna get rocky/We gonna move down to the next ya jockey now!*") ai contenuti visivi decisamente "kawai" – tra le altre cose, il nostro impara il karate da una cipolla, prepara una torta insieme ad una gallina, fa la fila per andare alla toilette e prende lezioni di guida da un'alce, l'irreprensibile Mooselini. Brani come "Chop Chop Master Onion's" o "Cheap Cheap The Cooking Chicken's" sono diventati dei classici. *Parappa The Rappa* ha figliato una serie animata trasmessa in prima serata dalla televisione nipponica Fuji Television nonché un clone [stra]fatto-in-casa, *Um Jammer Lammy* (PlayStation, 1997), "interpretato" da una simpatica chitarrista alle prime armi. Per quanto la componente grafica e i personaggi di *Um Jammer Lammy* siano ancora più surreali di quelli di Parappa, il comparto sonoro fastidiosamente rockeggiante ed un livello di difficoltà fin troppo elevato ne hanno compromesso il successo.

anticipated the portable electronic craze.

A few years later, the American software house Epyx released *Break Dance* (1984), a Commodore 64 videogame that required players to emulate the convoluted movements of virtual dancers. But the prototypical dance game was introduced by Nintendo in 1988, with the *Power Pad*, a mat equipped with sensors that could be linked to the NES console. The device allowed players to use their feet in order to interact with the onscreen characters. One of the few games that actually took advantage of the *Power Pad* is *Dance Aerobics*, an electronic simulation of the popular dance.

After a decade of highs and lows (most lows, admittedly), the dance music genre has literally exploded in the second half of the Nineties. Factors such as the emergence of the CD as the common format for music and games, the appearance of new consoles equipped with sophisticated sound chips combined with the funky imagination of Japanese game designers transformed a niche pastime in the 21st century karaoke.

Parappa and his brothers

The father of dance games is Masaya Matsuura. Born in June 1961 in Osaka, Japan and graduated from Ritsumeikan University with a major in industrial sociology, Matsuura fell in love with electronic music at the age of 19. An Apple II and a program called *Kaleidoscope* changed his life dramatically. After a ten-year long career in the music business – he was a member of the band *PYSYS* (pronounced "size"), which debuted in 1983 with the single "Different View" – Matsuura, experimented with interactive music. At the beginning of the Nineties, he produced a CD-ROM for the Macintosh titled *The Seven Colors*, followed by the equally brilliant *X-Tool*. But this volcanic *game designer*, leader maximo of Na-Na-Oh-Sha studio, achieved worldwide fame with *Parappa The Rappa* (PlayStation, 1996).

Thanks to an easy to learn back-and-forth repeating system - where the computer controlled character does a few bars of a rap and then the human player has to repeat them by hitting the buttons on the control pad – and a game style that simultaneously mimicked street culture and children books' illustration, *Parappa The*

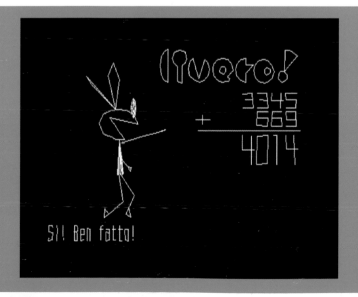

Basato sul medesimo meccanismo di *Parappa The Rappa*, *Vib Ribbon* (PlayStation, 1997) è, se possibile, ancora più bizzarro ed originale. Laddove il predecessore era caratterizzato da una grafica debordante e fumettosa, *Vib Ribbon* adotta uno stile grafico minimalista, in bianco e nero, caratterizzato da vettori monolineari. Un autentico omaggio ai videogiochi classici della fine degli anni settanta, da *Asteroids* a *Battle Zone*. Il protagonista è Vib un coniglietto fatto col filo di ferro che ricorda vagamente i personaggi del fumetto *Life In Hell* di Matt Groening. Al pari della "Linea", l'indimenticabile personaggio di Cavandoli, Vib procede lungo un nastro bianco che si modifica al ritmo della musica, nella fattispecie un pop bubblegum *à la* Fantastic Plastic Machine e Pizzicato Five. La pressione ritmica dei tasti del pad consente di schivare gli ostacoli che si presentano sul cammino, ma combinazioni di ostacoli vanno affrontate con la pressione combinata di più tasti. La collisione con una delle irregolarità geometriche della linea – loop, colonne, buche - ha conseguenze deleterie; Vib regredisce dal suo stadio di coniglio a forme di animale vettoriale inferiore. Viceversa, se Vib dimostra sufficiente tempismo può evolvere in forme superiori. La filosofia del gioco è chiaramente darwinista. Ciò che rende davvero irresistibile *Vib Ribbon* è che gli imprevedibili andamenti della linea sono generati in tempo reale dalla musica, il che significa che inserendo nel disc tray di PlayStation un qualunque CD audio, si ottengono nuovi *pattern*. Va da sè che oltre i 120 bpm, l'esperienza ludica diventa qualcosa di travolgente.

Dissimulazioni

L'evoluzione dei *dance game* ha assunto forme decisamente varie. Nel 1996 sono apparsi titoli-battistrada che hanno *de facto* contribuito ad stimolare l'attenzione della comunità videoludica. Tra questi è *Gaball Screen* (PlayStation, 1996), prodotto da Tetsuya Komuro ex-tastierista di TM Network. Il gioco, che si avvale dei vocalizzi di Utsonomiya Takashi, combina suoni, immagini ed oltre una trentina di "scenari tridimensionali esplorabili al ritmo di musica". Un secondo esempio è il bizzarro *Depht* (Sony Computer Entertainment), nel quale balene e delfini virtuali nuotano in un mare di note. Qui il giocatore può modificare le melodie per mezzo di un "Groove Editor" e mixare oltre 400 pattern sonori. Un'esperienza ludica mesmerizzante.

Il genere ludico musicale ha fatto le sue prime, timide apparizioni anche sotto le mentite spoglie delle simulazioni. Una di queste è *Debut 21* (PlayStation, 1997), nel quale il giocatore, nei panni di un producer discografico, ha un anno di tempo per trasformare una *teenager* qualunque in una pop star. Nel gioco prodotto da NEC, il producer deve pianificare con cura gli impegni della ragazza, indirizzarla verso la televisione piuttosto che la radio nonchè insegnarle

i rudimenti del ballo e della danza. Analogamente, in *Sold Out!* (PlayStation, 1997) prodotto da Shinko Music, il giocatore è un impresario di una banda rock, reggae oppure R&B. Tra gli obiettivi del gioco trovare i locali più fichi per suonare, promuovere gli album della band e soprattutto organizzare concerti.

Last Night a DJ Saved My Life

Nel frattempo, Sega pubblicava *Digital Dance Mix: Namie Amuro* (Saturn, 1997), un prodotto a metà tra il videoclip elettronico ed il videogioco. La virtual idoru Namie Amuro esegue una serie di brani ad uso e consumo di un'utenza decisamente "burusera" o fetish, per chi non mastica il

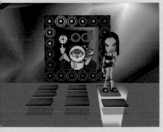

Rapper became an overnight cult. As a typical example of globalized entertainment, the PlayStation game lies at the intersection between East and West. Parappa is both a martial art champion and a rapping dog madly in love with a talking flower, Sunny Funny. The characters, created by Californian artist Rodney Alan Greenblat, don't hide their bi-dimensional nature behind an insane amount of polygons. On the contrary, they bend as if they were made of paper – incidentally, "parappa" means "flat" or "paper-thin" – and merrily dance in surreal stages. *Parappa The Rappa* is permeated by a demented humor, with its sticky lyrics *("Don't get cocky/It's gonna get rocky/We gonna move down to the next ya jockey now!")* and its "kawai"-looking visuals. Among other things, Parappa takes karate lessons from an onion, prepares a cake with a chicken, waits in line for the toilet and goes for a test drive with a moose, the irrepressible Mooselini. Tracks such as "Chop Chop Master Onion's" or "Cheap Cheap The Cooking Chicken's" have become instant-classics. *Parappa The Rapper* has its own primetime animated show on Fuji Television and an evil twin, *Um Jammer Lammy* (PlayStation, 1997), which stars a guitarist on her way to success. Despite a set of quirky characters and hip graphics that exceed Parappa's funkiness *Um Jammer Lammy*, the game failed commercially due to its frustrating difficulty level and a fastidious rock score.

Based on the same formula originally applied by *Parappa The Rappa*, *Vib Ribbon* (PlayStation, 1997) is, if possible, even zanier than the original. Whereas its predecessor was characterized by on over-the-edge comics-like visual style, *Vib Ribbon* uses minimalist graphics, e.g. black and white monolinear vectors. A true homage to classic videogames of the late Seventies, from *Asteroids* to *Battle Zone*. The protagonist is Vib, a wire-frame rabbit that vaguely resembles the characters of Matt Groening's *Life in Hell*. As "Linea", the unforgettable hero created by Italian artist Cavandoli, Vib walks along a white line that changes and reacts to the music, a mixture of bubblegum pop *à la* Fantastic Plastic Machine and Pizzicato Five. By pressing the buttons on the joypad in a timely manner, Vib can avoid the various obstacles that he find on its path, but a series of obstacles require more complex procedures. By getting to the end of each song, the game tabulates the score. Colliding with one of the obstructions - loops, pits, or columns - has deleterious consequences: Vib devolves from its rabbit-like stage to an inferior form. On the other hand, if Vib performs well, he can evolve into a superior creature. The game's philosophy is clearly Darwinist. What makes *Vib Ribbon* truly irresistible lies in the infinite variety of the levels' architecture: the patterns change in real time according to the melodies, therefore by inserting a different music CD into the PlayStation disc-tray is possible to embark new aural and visual trips. It goes without saying that anything beyond 120 bpm transforms the technoludic experience into something devastating.

Dissimulations

The evolution of dance games has assumed unexpected forms. In 1996, many video games foreshadowed the genre and titillated the audiences' interest. One of these products is *Gaball Screen* (PlayStation) produced by Tetsuya Komuro, former drummer of TM Network. The game, which benefits from Utsonomiya Takashi's vocals, combines sounds, images and more than thirty "3D environments that can be aurally explored". Another example is *Depth*, a bizarre game by Sony Computer Entertainment in which virtual whales and dolphins swim in a sea of music keys. The player can modify the melodies with the aide of a "Groove Editor" and mix more than 400 sound patterns. A mesmerizing experience. The music game genre also made its first, timid appearances, under the guise of life-simulations. For instance, in *Debut 21* (PlayStation, NEC, 1997) the player takes the role of a music producer and has one year to transform a teenager into

BUST A MOVE 2

giapponese. Pubblicato sull'ormai defunta console a 32-bit Sega, *DJ Wars* (Saturn, 1997) è invece un *rhytm* game del tutto peculiare. Una cinquina di DJ sintetici partecipano a gare di mixaggio nei nove club più esclusivi di Tokyo. Oltre al soundtrack esplosivo - cinquanta brani dance remixabili dall'utente - *DJ Wars* consentiva ai novelli deejay di attingere dalla propria collezione audio. Lo scarso successo della piattaforma Sega ha fortemente limitato la diffusione di *DJ Wars*, ma la medesima formula è stata ripresa - con qualche variante e con esiti del tutto differenti - da Konami.

Analogamente, le innovazioni introdotte dal rapper Sony sono state imitate ed implementate dal fior fiore delle software house nipponiche. Tra i cloni più interessanti spicca *Bust a Move* (PlayStation, 1998), conosciuto in occidente come *Bust a Groove* in Europa e Stati Uniti. Sviluppato da Metro Graphics e pubblicato da Enix, il gioco miscela elementi dei picchiaduro e del neo-nato genere video-musicale consentendo ad avatar tridimensionali di sfidarsi in incontri mozzafiato di ballo funky. A differenza di *Parappa The Rappa*, in cui il giocatore deve limitarsi a ripetere la sequenza di note selezionata dal computer, in *Bust A Move* l'azione si svolge in tempo reale. *Bust A Move* può essere considerato il primo vero simulatore di ballo per PlayStation. Personaggi memorabili, balletti esilaranti, animazioni in *motion capture* di ottima qualità e una colonna sonora irresistibile hanno trasformato il giochino di Metro Graphics in una vera e propria mania. In tempi più recenti, *Bust a Move* ha figliato un seguito, *Bust a Move 2* e una variante, *Dance Summit 2001*, che supporta sia i controller standard sia una speciale interfaccia.

Non Si Uccidono Così Anche I Cavalli?

Se non c'è dubbio che Parappa e *Bust a Move* abbiano posto le basi del genere dei *dance music*, è altrettanto vero che è stata Konami a dare avvio alla rivoluzione. L'etichetta nipponica ha sintetizzato i migliori elementi dei precedenti titoli enfatizzando la componente performativa e trasformando *de facto* il videogiocatore in un ballerino. Konami ha inaugurato la serie videomusicale conosciuta in Giappone come *Bemani*, un'evoluzione diretta dei karaoke ludici di etichette come Sega (si veda *Prologue 21*, basato su architettura Saturn, 1994) o la versione *on-demand* introdotta nel 1992 da Taito. Il capostipite dei Bemani è *Beatmania* (ribattezzato *Hip Hop Mania* negli Stati Uniti, 1997) che ha ripreso il tema di *DJ Wars* nel contesto dei cosiddetti *geimu sentah* o *geimusen*, le sale giochi nipponiche. Il coin-op originale era caratterizzato da un cabinato mostruosamente ingombrante dotato di una tastiera, coppia di piatti per lo scratching e uno speaker capace di assordare chiunque si fosse trovato nel raggio di trenta metri. Accompagnato da una selezione di brani che spaziano dalla musica classica al pop più commerciale di "Kung Fu Fighting" e Chumbawumba, senza dimenticare la disco nipponica di Captain Jack ed E-Rotic, *Beatmania* è in grado di soddisfare tutte le orecchie e di trasformare anche il più noioso ragioniere in un maniaco del mix. Va sottolineato che la qualità degli arrangiamenti varia considerevolmente e in alcuni casi si scade al livello di Cristina D'Avena. Lo straordinario successo di *Beatmania* ha spinto Konami ad introdurre innumerevoli varianti e remix, in versione arcade e per console, da PlayStation a Game Boy. Brani come "Dam Dariram", "Operator", "Do It All Night" "Dynamite Rave", senza dimenticare il disco sound italiano, hanno scalato le classifiche di vendita giapponesi. Dopo il quarto remix, Konami ha tentato di ridefinire l'esperienza con *Beatmania II*, fallendo su tutta la linea.

Nonostante uno schermo panoramico a cristalli liquidi, extra subwoofer e un pedale per gli effetti, il gioco ha perso in semplicità diventando estremamente frustrante. Non sorprende che con il quinto remix, sottotitolato *Love The Beat*, *Beatmania Club Mix* e soprattutto *Beatmania III* si sia ritornati alle origini...

Ma è stato il secondo titolo della serie Bemani a ridefinire il genere dei *dance game* tanto in Giappone quanto in Occidente: *Dance Dance Revolution* (1998), un coin-op dalle fattezze

BUST-A-GROOVE

a pop star. In this game, the producer must carefully plan the girl's schedule, chose between television rather than radio and teach her the fundamentals of dancing and singing. Similarly, in *Sold Out!* (PlayStation, 1997) by Shinko Music, the player is the manager of a rock, reggae or R&B band. Our tasks include cruising cities in search for the perfect venues, promote the band's musical efforts, and organize concerts.

Last Night a DJ Saved My Life

Meanwhile, Sega published a various array of bizarre titles for its ill-fated Saturn platform. Take *Digital Dance Mix: Namie Amuro* (1997), for instance, a product that is not really an interactive video clip nor a conventional videogames. Virtual idoru Namie Amuro performs a selection of songs for a "burusera" (Japanese for fetish) crowd. Equally peculiar is *DJ Wars* (1997), a rhythm game in which the five best Tokyo DJs compete for supremacy in the cutthroat Tokyo club scene. *DJ Wars* not only boosted a killer soundtrack – more than 50 remixable dance tracks – but also allowed players to make full use of their own audio collection in the game. Due to the lack of success of Sega's console, *DJ Wars*' popularity has been limited, but its formula can be found – with marginal differences – in Konami's *Beatmania* series. Analogously, the innovations introduced by Sony's rapper have been imitated and implemented in a variety of games. One of the most interesting clones is *Bust a Move* (PlayStation, 1998), known in the US and Europe as *Bust a Groove* for licensing reasons. Developed by Metro Graphics and published by Enix, the game combines elements from beat'em ups and video music genre allowing three-dimensional avatars to perform snazzy dance steps to popular music. While in *Parappa The Rappa* the player is limited to repeat a predetermined sequence of music keys, here the action takes place in real time. *Bust A Move* can be considered the first dance simulator for the PlayStation. Memorable characters, exhilarating ballets, excellent motion-captured

animations, and an irresistible soundtrack are just few of the reasons why Metro Graphics' game achieved a cult-like status. More recently, *Bust a Move* has spawned a sequel, *Bust a Move 2*, and a spin-off, *Dance Summit 2001*, which supports the standard controllers as well as a dedicated interface.

They Shoot Horses, Don't They?

Although it is hardly disputable that both *Parappa* and *Bust a Move* have established the conventions of the genre, it is equally true that Konami initiated the beat revolution. The Japanese company synthesized the best elements of the previous titles emphasizing the performance aspect and *de facto* redefining the player as a dancer.

Konami launched the video music series known in Japan as Bemani, a direct evolution of digital karaoke machines produced by Sega (see, for instance, the Saturn-based *Prologue 21*, 1994) or the on-demand version introduced by Taito in 1992. The first title in the Bemani series is *Beatmania* (also known as *Hip Hop Mania* in the US and Europe, 1997), a coin-op that took the *DJ Wars*' concept a step further. The game – which allowed players to simulate the experience of being a DJ - became a staple of the so-called *geimu sentah o geimusen*, literally game centers, the Japanese arcades. The original machines featured a huge cabinet equipped with a keyboard, a twin-set of simulated turntables for scratching and a powerful speaker. Accompanied by an assorted selection of tracks that ranged from classical music to commercial tunes such as "Kung Fu Fighting" and "Chumbawumba", not mentioning Nippon disco (Captain Jack and E-Rotic among the others), *Beatmania* offered endless aural pleasures, although it must be said that the quality level is rather heterogeneous. To maximize *Beatmania*'s extraordinary success, Konami introduced a plethora of sequels and remixed versions, both in the arcades and on domestic consoles like PlayStation and Game Boy. Songs like "Dam Dariram",

 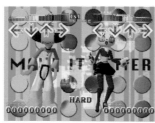   

elefantiache, leggi cabinato dotato di singolo schermo e affiancato da due piattaforme di ballo equipaggiate di sensori. Lo scopo del gioco è sempre quello: ripetere le sequenze di luci e suoni. Ma questa volta con i piedi (*guarda mamma, senza mani!*). *Dance Dance Revolution* – versione post-moderna del *Twister* e del *Simon* messi assieme - ha dato origine ad un autentico fenomeno pop culturale in Giappone, ingollando gettoni con inquietante rapidità ed efficienza. Ancora più sorprendentemente, il gioco ha riscosso un analogo successo anche negli Stati Uniti, dove sono stati istituiti competizioni di ballo elettronico a livello nazionale. Autentiche maratone non dissimili da quelle messe in scena da Sydney Pollack in *Non Si Uccidono Così Anche i Cavalli* (1969), nel quale il ballo perde ogni valenza artistica per diventare un massacrante esercizio fisico. Le conversioni casalinghe, dotate di tappetini muniti di sensori, hanno letteralmente spopolato. Sul piano aurale, *Dance Dance Revolution* vanta uno dei migliori accompagnamenti sonori nella storia dei videogiochi, una antologia spumeggiante che spazia dalla disco alla trance, dall'hip hop alla techno, punteggiata dai commenti bizzarri dello speaker virtuale (come "You are a dance animal" o "Fujiyamaaaaa!"). Dopo il successo del primo gioco, Konami ha stretto un accordo con Toshiba EMI per poter sfruttare nei bemani brani della scena club nipponica. Analogamente, Konami ha stretto un accordo con Universal Music per ottenere la licenza di brani di band popolari come Boyzone da includere nella versione europea di *Dance Dance Revolution, Dancing Stage Euromix I*. In due anni, l'etichetta nipponica ha venduto qualcosa come 15,000 cabinati e 3 milioni di copie delle versioni da casa, senza contare le 800,000 copie del soundtrack. Impressionante, poi la sequela di seguiti e spin-off, da *Guitar Freaks* a *Drummania*, da *Keyboardmania* a *Pop'N Music*, ciascuno caratterizzato da uno speciale controller (chitarra elettrica, percussioni, tastiere e così via). Altre varianti includono *True Kiss Destination*, che si avvale del contributo del producer Tetsuya Komuro, *Dance Dance Revolution Solo Mix*, che include un'interfaccia di controllo più complessa ed un numero incalcolabile di *Club Mix* per PlayStation, con brani tratti da cartoni animati come *Occhi di Gatto* e *Lupin III*. L'ultima follia di Konami è *Para Para Paradise* (2001), un gioco da bar dotato di speciali sensori che rivelano il movimento delle braccia dei ballerini impegnati nel Para Para, un nuovo stile di ballo che privilegia i movimenti del torso e delle braccia. Il prossimo passo? Combinare il gameplay di *Dance Dance Revolution* a quello di *Para Para Paradise*, per creare il simulatore di ballo completo.

DANCE DANCE REVOLUTION

"Operator", "Do It All Night" "Dynamite Rave", not forgetting Italian disco, have dominated the Japanese charts for months. After the 4th Remix, Konami tried to redefine the experience with a true sequel, *Beatmania II*, but failed miserably. Despite the huge LCD screen, an extra subwoofer and a foot pedal for special sound effects, the game was disappointingly complicated and ultimately frustrating. It comes as no surprise, thus, that Konami decided to go back to the roots with the 5th Remix, subtitled *Love The Beat*, *Beatmania Club Mix* and especially *Beatmania III*…

But it's Bemani's second game that truly reinvented the genre, both in Japan and in Western countries: *Dance Dance Revolution* (1998). The game sported a gigantic cabinet equipped with two dancing platforms. The aim of the game did not change a bit: the player must repeat correctly the sequence of lights and sounds. But this time, he has to use his feet (*Look, ma, no hands!*). In short, the game requires dancer-players to synchronize their dance movements on the marked floor pad with flashing arrows on the machine's screen, in single or pairs. *Dance Dance Revolution* – a post-modern game that combines both *Twister* and *Simon* – gave birth to a new cultural phenomenon in Japan and single-handedly rescued the stagnating arcade market by becoming the top single token-devourers. Even more surprisingly, the game obtained a similar success in the US: as soon as *Dance Dance Revolution* was introduced, the players spontaneously organized a myriad of tournaments and competitions, not unlike those depicted in Sydney Pollack's *They Shoot Horses, Don't They?* (1969). The movie recreated one of the many barbaric dance marathons of the 30s: in both cases, dance is deprived of its artistic value and becomes a grueling physical exercise (it's not by chance that some versions include a Diet Mode with a calories counter, in pure treadmill fashion). Aurally speaking, *Dance Dance Revolution* offers one of the greatest musical score ever: a vibrating anthology that ranges from disco to trance, from hip hop to techno, punctuated by a series of bizarre comments from the speaker ("*You are a dance animal*" or "*Fujiyamaaaaa!*"). Konami has also signed an agreement with Toshiba EMI to use disco tracks in its games. Similarly, the Japanese software house has obtained the rights to use popular songs from Universal Music (Boyzone's and the like) in the European versions of *Dance Dance Revolution*, titled *Dancing Stage Euromix*. In less than two years, Konami

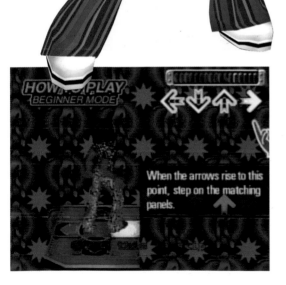

When the arrows rise to this point, step on the matching panels.

Electric Barbarella

Dal 1999, il genere dei *music games* monopolizza la scena ludica nipponica, specialmente per quanto concerne il segmento arcade. Ma laddove Konami ha scelto la via della "simulazione totale", riproducendo in forma elettronica le dinamiche del ballo, aziende come Sega e Tecmo hanno scelto di privilegiare la componente estetica dei giochi. Prendiamo *Space Channel 5* (2000) e *Samba De Amigo* (2000), entrambi pubblicati da Sega. Il primo, apparso originariamente su Dreamcast, segna un marcato ritorno alla formula *à là Simon* di *Parappa The Rappa* ed è indubbiamente uno dei giochi piu' rifiniti dal punto di vista cosmetico della storia dei videogames. Creato dal veterano programmatore Tetsuya Mizuguchi, leader di United Game Artists, il gioco è "interpretato" da Ulala, una Barbarella iper-sexy in minigonna di latex digitale. La splendida giornalista spaziale si trova a fare i conti con una cospirazione aliena. I moloriani, buffa razza extraterrestre, stanno infatti contagiando l'umanità con la febbre del boogie. Per salvare la Terra la nostra eroina deve ballare contro gli alieni. In altre parole, il futuro della razza umana è riposto tutto nelle sue anche. Il *gameplay* è incredibilmente semplice: gli avversari eseguono un paio di mosse che il giocatore deve imitare premendo correttamente i tasti sul pad. Se si riesce nell'impresa gli ostaggi verranno liberati e gli alieni saranno spazzati via. Allo stesso tempo, la propria performance influenzerà gli ascolti televisivi del canale di Ulala: mancate il ritmo e il vostro show verrà cancellato. *Space Channel 5* si ispira ad una psichedelia degli anni sessanta filtrata da Austin Powers e si avvale di una colonna sonora che spazia dal jap-pop più plasticoso alla trance. Ma nonostante le animazioni da cartone animato e cromatismi da triplo attacco epilettico, *Space Channel 5* è passato praticamente inosservato in Giappone e Ulala è diventata tutto fuorchè un'icona pop. Sega spera di rimediare con i nuovi episodi in arrivo per Xbox, Sony PlayStation2 e Dreamcast. Resta il fatto che la proliferazione di eroi e di eroine dei *dance games* rappresenta un'ulteriore segnale del trionfo del simulacro baudrillardiano. Al pari della virtual pop-star Kyoko Date e delle bambole kisekae su internet, un personaggio come Ulala conferma che stiamo procedendo verso la progressiva smaterializzazione della celebrità. Ha avuto decisamente più fortuna il coloratissimo *Samba De Amigo* (coin-op, Dreamcast, 2000), un rythm-game tremendamente coinvolgente che ha debuttato in sala giochi con un bel paio di sofisticate maracas elettroniche da scuotere al ritmo della musica e da un tappetino dotato di sensori atti a rilevare il loro movimento. Scimmie ballerine, personaggi fumettosi, beats latineggianti ed

SAMBA DE AMIGO

has sold more than 15,000 machines and 3 million units of the console versions, not forgetting more than 800,000 copies of the soundtrack. Many of the musical artists in the *Dance Dance Revolution* series have actually gone on to have successful careers in no small part because of the game itself. The original title has been followed by oh-so-many sequels and variants, such as *Guitar Freaks*, *Drummania*, *Keyboardmania*, and *Pop'N Music*, each characterized by a special interface (electric guitar, drums, keyboards and so on). Other titles are *True Kiss Destination* – which features Tetsuya Komuro - *Dance Dance Revolution Solo Mix*, equipped by an even more complex controller, and an impressive assortment of *Club Mix* for the Sony PlayStation which includes tracks from popular anime such as *Cat's Eye* and *Lupin the Third*. Konami's latest title, *Para Para Paradise* (2001) senses arm movements to simulate the popular Para Para dancing style that is currently sweeping the country. The next step? A game that will mingle the arm-sensing movements of *Para Para Paradise* with the foot action of *Dance Dance Revolution*, creating a full-body dance experience. The ultimate simulation.

Electric Barbarella

By 1999, the *music games* genre were monopolizing the Japanese arcade scene. Whilst Konami strove to fully recreate the dance experience with the aid of technology and to find new means to immerse players in the experience on offer, companies such as Sega and Tecmo tended to privilege the visual component of the games. Both *Space Channel 5* (1999) and *Samba De Amigo* (2000), both published by Sega, display weird yet ultimately highly stylized aesthetics. The former, originally published on Dreamcast, present a gameplay similar to *Parappa*'s but on the graphics side is a totally different ballgame. Created by veteran programmer Tetsuya Mizuguchi, United Game Artists' director, the game features Ulala, an hyper-sexy Barbarella who wears a digital latex miniskirt. The gorgeous journalist is facing an alien conspiracy. After a weird alien race, the Molorians, invades a local spaceport Ulala heads in armed with cameras and laser guns, determined to report the news while obliterating the alien scum. As she makes her way through the space station, aliens pop out from every possible angles. The aim of the game is to mimic their movements and force them to succumb to Ulala's substantially superior dancing skills and stylistic sense. In other words, the destiny of the human race lies between her hips. If Ulala makes a wrong move, the humans will succumbs. Even worse, her TV show will be cancelled. *Space Channels 5*'s aesthetics are clearly influenced by 60s psychedelics, filtered by *Austin Powers*' irony. The soundtrack, on the other hand, comprises a selection that ranges from plastic-like Japanese pop to contemporary trance. But despite cartoon-like animations and the triple-epileptic attack chromatic choices, *Space Channel 5* was mainly ignored in Japan. Ulala has yet to become a pop icon such as Lara Croft, but Sega is currently at work to fix the situation. New episodes are due soon on Dreamcast, Xbox, and PlayStation2. Nonetheless, the proliferation of dance heroes and heroines confirms that the Baudrillardian simulacra are taking over. The symbolism of dance routines has entered the realm of the hyper-real. Just like virtual pop star such as Kyoko Date and the kisekae dolls on the Internet, Ulala is the prototype of the fantasmatic celebrity.

The brainchild of Sonic Team's veteran Yuki Naka, *Samba De Amigo* (coin-op, Dreamcast), not only impressed the critics but also achieved a commercial success. The game debuted in the arcades with a pair of electronic maracas. The highly involving rhythm game was also equipped with a

SPACE CHANNEL FIVE

un gameplay irresistibile rendono il gioco di Yuki Naka, leader di SonicTeam, un *tour-de-force* audiovisuale. Si noti che la versione da casa include anche remix delle colonne sonore di coin-op d'annata come *Out Run* ed *Afterburner*. Tutt'altro che sorprendentemente, *Samba De Amigo* ha figliato un seguito e numerosi cloni, tra cui *Shaker & Tamburine* (2001), che include un tamburello al posto delle maracas.

Nel tentativo di cavalcare l'onda lunga del genere videoludico musicale etichette minori hanno prodotto titoli come *Cool Cool Toon* (SNK, Arcade & Dreamcast), *Puyo Puyo Da!* (Compile), *Goo! Goo! Soundy & Kitty the Kool!* (PlayStation), *GuitaruMan One* (Koei), *Punch the Monkey Game Edition* (la versione dance di *Lupin III*), *Technictix* (Akira, PlayStation2) *Stepping Selection 1 & 2* (Jaleco, PlyStation 2, Arcade), *Maestromusic* (Global A Entertainment, PlayStation, 1999 - che consente di diventare un direttore d'orchestra) nonchè *Unison: Rebels of Rhythm and Dance* (Tecmo, un insano incrocio tra *Footloose* e *Space Channel 5*), variamente accolti dal pubblico. In molti casi, le software house si sono limitate ad riciclare nei loro dance games personaggi già apparsi in altre serie.

I Want My TVDJ

Il genere dei *music games* si sta evolvendo in modo rapido ed imprevedibile, dando luogo a curiose ibridazioni. Una di queste è *TVDJ* (PlayStation2, 2001). Prodotto da Sony Computer Entertainment, il gioco ci mette nei panni di un DJ televisivo, in arte VJ, impegnato a risollevare le sorti di un canale televisivo in crisi di audience. Sul piano estetico, *TVDJ* utilizza la medesima tecnica di *Jet Grind Radio* (Dreamcast, 2000), *cell-shading*, che consiste nel ritoccare con una marcata linea nera i contorni dei personaggi in modo da distinguerli nettamente dal *background*. Questa tecnica, unita all'uso di colori vibranti, rende il videogioco esteticamente simile ad cartone animato. La meccanica di gioco, tuttavia, non è molto differente da quella di *Parappa*. Ad aggravare le cose, la non perfetta sincronia tra beat e azione sullo schermo. In una sola parola, migliorabile.

SPACE CHANNEL FIVE

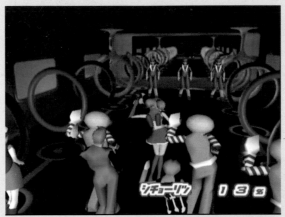

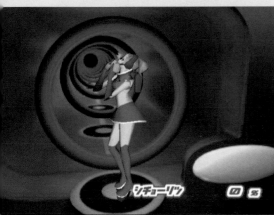

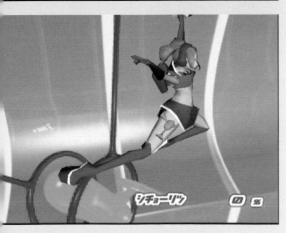

sensory-filled mat. Motion-sensing technology to sense the position of each maraca (which must be shaken to the beat either high, medium, or low), dancing monkeys, comic-like characters, Latin beats and an irresistible gameplay allowed Naka's game to become one of Sega's greatest hits in years. An audiovisual *tour de force*, *Samba De Amigo* also featured remixed versions of classic coin-ops such as *Out Run* and *Afterburner*. Quite predictably, the game spawned a sequel and many clones, like *Shaker & Tambourine* (2001), that replaced the maracas with... yep, a tambourine.

Riding the tsunami of Japanese music-themed action games, minor game companies produced an immense set of titles. Worthy of mentioning are *Cool Cool Toon* (SNK, Arcade & Dreamcast), *Puyo Puyo Da!* (Compile), *Goo! Goo! Soundy & Kitty the Kool!* (PlayStation), *GuitaruMan One* (Koei), *Punch the Monkey Game Edition* (dance version of the popular anime *Lupin III*), *Technictix* (Akira, PlayStation2) *Stepping Selection 1 & 2* (Jaleco, PlayStation 2, Arcade), *Maestromusic* (Global A Entertainment, PlayStation, 1999 – a music conductor simulator!), and *Unison: Rebels of Rhythm and Dance* (Tecmo, an odd fusion of *Footloose* and *Space Channel 5*), differently welcomed by the public. In many cases, software houses simply recycled their mascot into the new music games.

Want My TVDJ!

The *music game* genre is evolving rapidly and unpredictably, often generating bizarre imbrications. Take, for instance, *TVDJ* (PlayStation2, 2001). Produced by Sony Computer Entertainment, the game features a televised DJ, *pardon*, a VJ, trying to improve the network's abysmal ratings. Cosmetically, *TVDJ* uses the same *cell-shading* techniques found in *Jet Grind Radio* (Dreamcast, 2000), that consists in drawing black lines around a character composed of polygons. The result is a hand drawn look-alike style. This process, enriched by the use of vibrant colors, transforms the videogame in a cartoonesque experience. Regardless of the originality of the visuals, the gameplay is unreservedly conventional and the not-so-perfect synchronicity between beats and action on the screen ruined an otherwise interesting game. Today, Japanese game centers replete with zany dance games like *Pump It Up!* (Andamiro, Arcade), *Flash Beats* (Sega, 2000) and *Tuba Freaks* (Konami, 2001). The latter, as the title suggests, is a tuba simulator. The tagline, "*Blow to the beat!*"

Le sale da gioco nipponiche, intanto, traboccano di *dance games* sempre più bizzarri come *Pump It Up!* (Andamiro, Arcade), *Flash Beats* (Sega, 2000) e *Tuba Freaks* (Konami, 2001). Quest'ultimo, incredibile a dirsi, è un simulatore di tuba. La *tagline*, "*Blow to the beat! This is the funky tuba style*", la dice tutta. Il giocatore si siede su uno sgabello e preme tre pulsanti collocati sulla tuba elettronica in corrispondenza ai simboli che compaiono sullo schermo. Il gioco ha riscosso un successo tale da spingere Namco a proporre immediatamente la sua versione, *Tuba No Tomodachi* (in giapponese, "gli amici della tuba"), dotato di un'interfaccia ancora più sofisticata. Al che Sega ha risposto introducendo *Dream Audition*, a metà tra il jukebox ed il karaoke.

In un prossimo futuro, i *dance games* saranno disponibili anche per telefoni cellulari. Konami ha infatti annunciato il servizio *Dancing Karaoke D Kara* che consentirà agli utenti di utilizzare la tastiera del proprio cellulare per giocare alla versione portatile di *Dance Dance Revolution*. I brani musicali potranno essere dowloadati per pochi yen dal sito Konami Music Online, che include oltre 16,000 canzoni.

In altre parole, non c'è scampo.

Disco Inferno

Nati come un passatempo per pochi fanatici, oggi i *music video games* sono diventati una vera e propria mania: sono usciti dal ghetto delle sale giochi per colonizzare il *mainstream*. Può sembrare in qualche modo sorprendente che in una cultura che ha fatto della discrezione un imperativo categorico, un'attività così esibizionista abbia raggiunto una simile popolarità. Ma come insegna il karaoke, quando si tratta di cantare e ballare, i giapponesi non si tirano mai indietro e devono *issho-kemmei ni yatta*, ossia "provarci". I *dance games* soddisfano il desiderio primordiale degli utenti di interagire con la musica, un linguaggio che trascende ogni cultura, come ha illustrato *Incontri Ravvicinati del Terzo Tipo* (1977) di George Lucas. I *rhythm games* hanno inoltre segnato una decisa rottura nei confronti della natura tradizionalmente statica della pratica videoludica introducendo l'elemento della *performance* e di un articolato coinvolgimento fisico. Inoltre, a differenza dei convenzionali videogiochi che richiedono una coordinazione occhio-mano, questo genere di prodotti coinvolgono anche l'orecchio. Le ultime incarnazioni dei *dance games* hanno un forte *appeal* anche sul pubblico femminile: così come l'utenza dei karaoke-bar è per un buon 60% femminile, allo stesso modo le donne ormai considerano le *geimu sentah* valide alternative alle discoteche, come testimonia il video *Temperamental* di Everything But The Girl.

Da Flash Gordon a Flashdance, il passo è breve.

UNISON

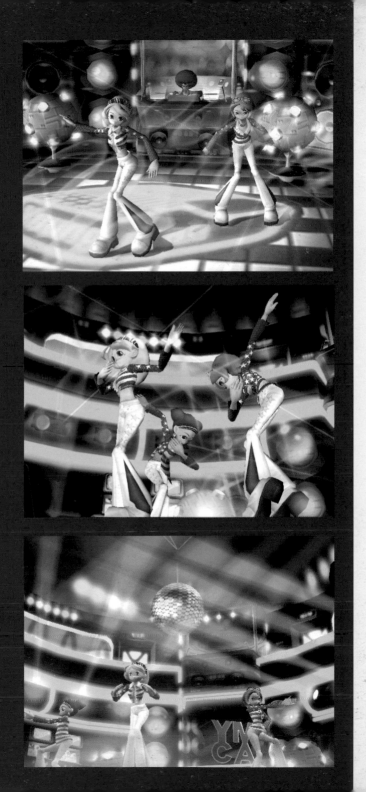

This is the *funky tuba style*", does not need additional comments. The player sits on a stool attached to the cabinet and pushes the buttons of the electronic tuba in order to match the corresponding symbols on the screen. The game was so successful that Namco, Sega's archrival, promptly introduced its version, *Tuba No Tomodachi* (literally "Tuba's Friends" in Japanese), which boosted an even more sophisticated interface. Sega's reply was *Dream Audition*, an hybrid jukebox-karaoke game.

And soon, dance games will be available through cellular phones as Konami is about to introduce a new service called *Dancing Karaoke D Kara*. Users will be able to use their phones' keyboard to play the portable versions of *Dance Dance Revolution*. New tunes could be downloaded for a fistful of yen from Konami's Music Online website, that will offer more than 16,000 tracks.

Bottom line: there is no way out.

Disco Inferno

What was once a niche pastime has now become a mainstream leisure-time favorite. In short, dance games have moved out of the otaku ghetto to occupy a relevant part of Japanese's life. It may seem strange that the Japanese - a culture that enlists "discretion" among its categorical imperatives – embraced this exhibitionistic activity with such an enthusiasm. On the other hand, this is a civilization raised on karaoke: when it comes to singing and dancing, the Japanese *issho-kemmei ni yatta*, "they must give it a good try". The appeal of *dance games* is not limited to males, but females as well. As with karaoke, whose audience is up to 60% female, these products are often played by girls. Beat games tap into instincts for rhythm and the primordial desire to interact with music, the universal language (as exemplified by George Lucas's *Close Encounters of The Third Kind*, 1977). They also broke down the traditionally static nature of gaming interaction by introducing a performance element and a full body involvement. If traditional video games require an hand-eye coordination, dance games also stimulate the ear. As Everything But The Girl's *Temperamental* video showed, the dance games are transforming the *geimu sentah* in valid alternatives to clubs.

Shall we dance?

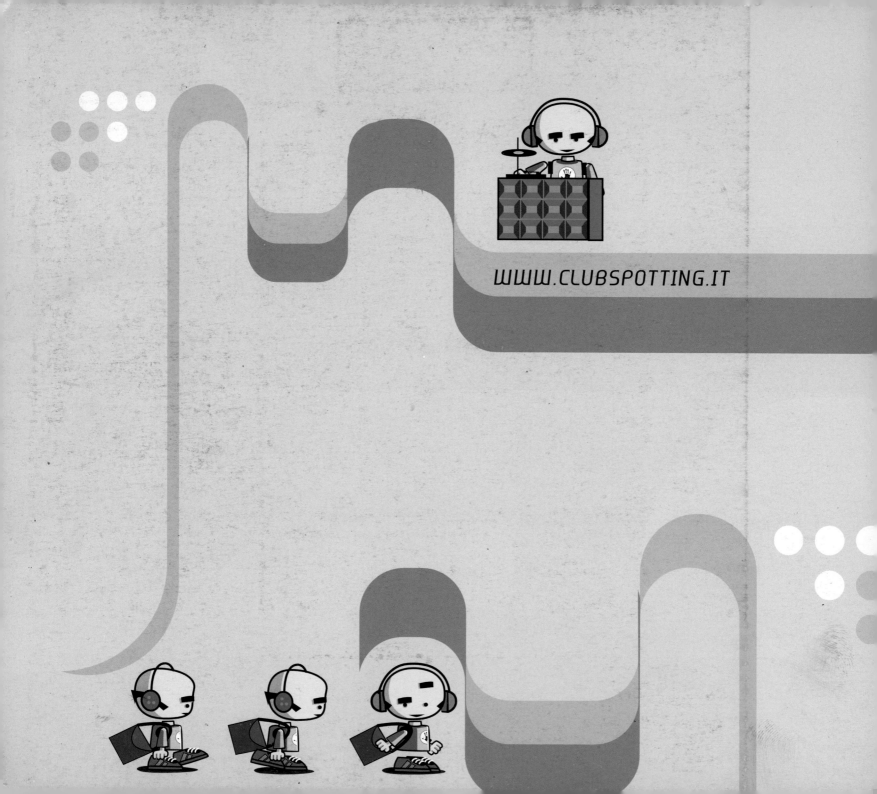

WWW.CLUBSPOTTING.IT